For Barbara
♡
Polly P. Stramm

SASSY, SWEET & SILLY
Southernisms

Polly Powers Stramm

Globe
Pequot

Guilford, Connecticut

Globe
Pequot

An imprint of The Rowman & Littlefield Publishing Group, Inc.
4501 Forbes Blvd., Ste. 200
Lanham, MD 20706
www.rowman.com

Distributed by NATIONAL BOOK NETWORK

British Library Cataloguing in Publication Information available

Library of Congress Cataloging-in-Publication Data available

ISBN 978-1-4930-3420-8 (hardcover)
ISBN 978-1-4930-3421-5 (e-book)

♾ The paper used in this publication meets the minimum requirements of American National Standard for Information Sciences—Permanence of Paper for Printed Library Materials, ANSI/NISO Z39.48-1992

Printed in the United States of America

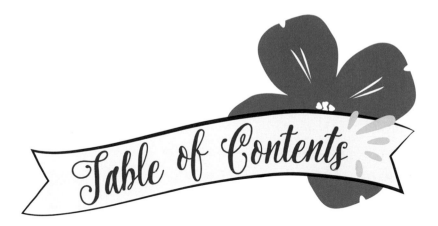

Table of Contents

Preface

When I was asked by my editor at the Globe Pequot Press if I could write a book about Southernisms, I said, "**Yes'm, I reckon** I can pull together a few hundred sayin's, stories, customs, and rituals in **two shakes of a billy goat's tail.**"

Of course, I don't claim to know every **cotton-pickin'** Southern sayin', expression, cliché, or adage, so that's why I figured I'd call on friends and family to share theirs with me. At first, most everybody I mentioned this assignment to said they couldn't think of anything off the tops of their heads, and then—**faster than greased lightning**— they'd say somethin' that fit the bill. Usually, they'd get tickled, bust a gut, and shrug their shoulders. These sayin's are so ingrained in Southern conversation, most of us don't realize they're sayin's.

That's a little bit of how this book came to be. It's a conglomeration of cooperation among friends, relatives, coworkers, my doctor, my dentist, and even the woman who handled my mammogram. I blabbed to everyone with whom I came in contact and—**faster than a windmill in a tornado**—a whole passel of texts, phone calls, and e-mails started comin' my way and didn't stop even after I sent the pages off to my editor.

Southerners are generous souls, and the **proof is in the puddin'** in this book. I extend a hearty thank-you to everyone who contributed their two cents to this book in any form or fashion. I'm **pleased as punch** that the opportunity was presented to me.

Now go on, y'all, turn the dadgum page.

Introduction

I swanee! What I'm about to tell y'all is the honest-to-gosh truth. When I was a student at the University of Georgia, I registered for an elective course called Introduction to Speech Communication. As part of the requirements, my classmates and I were required to give three talks, with the first being a speech to inform. I came up with the brilliant idea of enlightenin' my fellow classmates—all of whom **didn't know me from Adam's housecat**—with a few colorful expressions and how they came to be. To grab the attention of my audience, I started out with this confession: "I was caught with my pants down, but don't tell it to the Marines."

Sure enough, their attention was grabbed. To this day, I'm not exactly sure what they thought of this whippersnapper from southeast Georgia who shocked the livin' daylights out of each and everybody in that classroom. But I do know this: we Southerners have always had both our own vocabulary and a particular way of talkin', and more often than not, our gabfests involve humor. Sure, we might toss around an expression that people from other regions use, but you can count on us to tweak it a bit or sprinkle in a couple of descriptive words to make it pure Southern style.

We take our sweet time with everything, especially the way we talk. We may, on occasion, add far too many descriptive words when a few will be just fine and dandy. In the South, somethin' is not only good, it's also mighty good. Instead of takin' a minute, a task may take one doggone minute. When it's time to go, we might skedaddle after we say, "**OK then, bye now**"; if we want a kiss or a hug, we may ask someone to "**gimme some suga'**" or "**lemme hug your neck**"; and when we're **mad as a wet hen**, we might say "**durnit**" instead of a dreaded curse word that might embarrass our mamas. We understand that if we do dish out some sass, our daddy might tan our hides with a switch that he told us to cut out back.

Speakin' of dishes, we know all too well about grub, manners, and the Good Book. We grew up readin' books penned by Southern writers who introduced us to all kinds of characters, and we still watch television programs and movies made by Hollywood-types—**bless their hearts**—who think they know what Southerners say and how they act. Truth be told, they **don't know a hill of beans** about this place we call home.

I grew up hearin' and speakin' Southern and continue to use expressions and words with unique inflections that I have heard all my born days. My goal was to make this book both extra special and one that might bring a big ol' grin to a reader's face. Mostly, I wanted to educate people far and wide about Southern-speak and the delightful—and sometimes ornery—folks behind those colorful expressions.

ENJOY IT NOW, YA HEAR?

WHAT IN BLUE BLAZES DOES IT MEAN TO Speak Southern?

Dialects Cover the Region Like Grandma's Patchwork Quilt

The region in the United States known as the Deep South is as diverse as all get out. Put on your thinkin' cap and picture in your head Spanish moss–draped oaks in Georgia, mysterious bayous filled with cypress knees in Louisiana, majestic mountains in North Carolina, and miles of pristine beaches in South Carolina. Just the geography alone will work your brain so much you might think that you're not playin' with a full deck of cards.

The differences in both the lay of the land and the cultures throughout the South have resulted in sayin's, expressions, customs, and traditions that are **spread out all over like a cold pat of butter on a hot buttermilk biscuit.** But at the same time, most of us Southerners say y'all (you all) and yonder, leave our *g*'s off the ends of words, and smash words together like what'cha (what are you).

To make matters a teensy bit more confusin', bunches of Southernisms can be peculiar to a particular state but different in a city within that state. Take Charleston, South Carolina, for instance. Old-school Charlestonians omit the *r* in words like "smart" (smaht) or their hometown (Chahlston). Other residents of the South Carolina Lowcountry might pronounce the *r* in words but say others like boat as bo-et, reflecting the influence of Gullah or Geechee dialects that can be found in South Carolina as well as in the Sea Islands of Georgia. Both Gullah and Geechee date to the days when slaves from West Africa were brought to the United States. The dialects are thought to be a sort of jumbled-up mixture of English and African, and words include "chern" (children), "hangry" (hungry), and "wit" (with). In Savannah, Georgia, where I'm from, you might hear some people speak Geechee while others have a charmin' old Savannah accent and say things like "hoose" (house) and "a-boot" (about).

Louisiana—pronounced LOOZ-i-ana by those'n who live there and others in the South—is another first-rate example where language backgrounds reach way back to when the state was settled by the French. Meanwhile, Cajuns migrated south from the Acadia region of Canada to Louisiana and mixed in unique customs and lively words that can make you believe you're visitin' a foreign country. Listen to these examples: a Cajun with wanderlust is known to roday, and the mouse is their version of the tooth fairy. Think of bowls of jambalaya or okra gumbo and, dollars to donuts, your mind will conjure up a Cajun. If someone says they're gonna put a gris-gris on you, you'd better watch out. Gris-gris is a voodoo word that's used when people want to kid around, such as, "Your mama's gonna put the gris-gris on you." If you hear about the holy trinity in Louisiana, especially in Cajun country, it's not a church-related matter. The holy trinity of Cajun cookin' is bell peppers, onions, and celery. The word "dressed" doesn't necessarily mean your mama has on her pearls and her Sunday-go-to-meetin' clothes and is headin' out the door for church services. In Louisiana, the term "dressed" means you want your sandwich with all the fixin's, including mayonnaise, lettuce, tomatoes, and pickles

Funny, ain't it? And I'm not thinkin' *ha ha* funny; I mean funny as in different.

People from the Appalachian Mountains, a range that passes through Georgia, North Carolina, and Tennessee, among other states, also have their own way of communicatin' that can be plumb hard to figure. If a mountaineer is tired, he may be tarred, or if he's huntin' for a chaw of chewing tobacco, he's searching for a wad of bacca. Those from Appalachia also tend to put an *h* in front of certain words, such as "it."

When I was a child, my family spent a week or so every summer in the mountains of western North Carolina around a dot on the map called Bat Cave. We didn't stay in a motel (not sure there was one) because Mama and Daddy wanted us children to stay all together instead of in a couple of cookie-cutter, overpriced motel rooms. That's why we crowded into quaint little cabins alongside ice-cold mountain streams. No swimmin' pools, televisions, or fancy furniture. That was back in the day when family members talked to one another. Imagine that!

I remember sleepin' late one morning (if I recall, my cot was set up in the kitchen) and hearin' the housekeeper (an older mountain lady) open the door and, when she realized the cabin wasn't vacant, declaring, "I'm afeard hit's a stayover." I imagine that same woman would have said she might be plannin' to bake up some catheads (large biscuits) for supper or wantin' to give her son a wallop if he decided to lay out of school (play hooky).

Over yonder in Tennessee, Jack isn't just a name—it's the best damn whiskey you've ever had, accordin' to folks from that state. And in Nashville, which is nicknamed the buckle of the Bible Belt, good ol' Southern fried chicken is hot chicken and country is music. In Georgia—the largest state east of the Mississippi River—you'll find mountain dialects in the northern part of the state, country talkin' in southwest Georgia, and like I said before, Geechee and Gullah along the coastal areas.

Other words that are peculiar to particular states include:

- ## POKE SACK (A brown paper bag)

  *"Hey, young fella, how about loadin' my groceries in a **poke sack.**"*

- ## AIM (Plan to)

  *"I **aim** to go out to the farm and pick some cucumbers so I can put up some pickles for the church bazaar."*

- ## PLUM OR PLUMB (Completely)

  *"Her mama and daddy are **plumb** crazy, so it's no wonder she's a little bit wonky."*

- ## TEA (Iced and sweet)

  *"Kathleen? How 'bout pourin' Thomas a tall glass of **tea** to go along with his North Carolina barbecue and slaw."*

- ## KUDZU (A vine that grows in the South, among other places, that tends to overtake houses, trees, and most anything else in its path)

  *"Grandmama's old homeplace up in the country is about to fall down it's covered with so much **kudzu.**"*

- ## WHISTLE PIG (Ground hog)

  *"On February second, the **whistle pig** over by the Joneses' farm might see its shadow."*

- ## TOW SACK (Burlap bag)

  *"Hey, Uncle Joe. How 'bout puttin' some firewood in that **tow sack** out by the barn?"*

- ## NARY (None)

  *"**Nary** a soul was standin' outside in that frog strangler (pouring rain)."*

- ## BEAUTY PARLOR (Hair salon)

  *"Mama and her sister go to the **beauty parlor** every Tuesday for a wash and set and a bit of gossip on the side."*

- ## THE PIG (The Piggly Wiggly grocery store)

  *"Emma? Take me down to **the Pig** so I can pick up some sweet 'taters."*

- ## POKEY-DOTTED (Polka-dotted)

  *"Jenny is dyin' to have a **pokey-dotted** Easter dress."*

- ## GRITS (A Southern food staple)

  *"I'd like a couple of scrambled eggs, a side of bacon, and a bowl of cheese **grits,** please, ma'am."*

- ## GRITS (Acronym that stands for "Girls Raised in the South")

  *"I'd pay big money for one of those **GRITS** ball caps."*

- ## HOEDOWN, SHINDIG, OR PIG PICKIN'
  (A gatherin' of friends usually centered around food)

  *"I'm plannin' to go to the **shindig** on Roberts Road with all the girls from school."*

- ## SOWFF CAKA LACKEY (South Carolina)

  *"When I told them Jack was from **Sowff Caka Lackey**, they said he must be some kinda hick."*

Some folks mistakenly toss everyone in the South in the same pot, which is downright wrong. There are three distinct types of folks below the Mason-Dixon Line: the true Southerner, the hillbilly, and the redneck. Land sakes, I shouldn't even have to explain the difference between those fellas! Knowin' who's who in the South is easy as pie. Simply put, a Southerner has class. Period, 'nuf said. Sadly, folks who live elsewhere in the US of A might inaccurately label a Southerner as either a hillbilly or a redneck, and if they do, they're not actin' like they've got good sense. While a true Southerner would never park his truck on the grass in the front yard, a hillbilly might. A redneck, on the other hand, would proudly display his beat-up old truck without tires in his yard on concrete blocks. A Yankee is an entirely different sort. According to my husband, who was born and reared in New Jersey (I've been tryin' to train him and get him to see the light for more than twenty years), being a Yankee is "a serious malady afflicting those born north of the Mason-Dixon Line. Despite significant resistance [and this is direct quote from a true Yankee], the disorder has gradually drifted south and is carried primarily by retirees and directly impacts many Southern communities. The long-standing remedy for an outbreak of Yankeeism, which tends to increase during tropical storms and hurricanes, has been largely unsuccessful. Oftentimes when such events occur and massive evacuations to the north take place, more Yankees actually return to the South than left in the first place, thus exacerbating the problem."

Looks like I've got him on the right track. As my friend Mary Alice would say, "There's no sucha thing as Northern fried chicken or Northern hospitality."

Y'ALL OUGHT'N GO OUT IN THAT
Frog Strangler

Crazy Contractions and Made-Up Words

Beg your pardon if I'm repeatin' myself, but it goes without sayin' that genuine Southerners tend to make up words, incorporate old-fashioned terms in conversations, change the meanin' willy-nilly, pronounce words funny, and add to sentences somethin' awful. In fact, what you just read is typical of words a Southerner might use that sound different from those uttered in other parts of the country. "**Somethin' awful**," when used as an adverb, certainly isn't bad or unpleasant. At the same time in the South, "awful" can be defined as good, just as the words "**mighty**" or "**right**," when uttered by a Southerner, can mean extra special (as in, "She has a mighty fine personality and a right smart way of doin' things"). While others might set a table, Southerners set a spell or set about to do somethin'—but they also can set a mighty fine table.

Southern contractions also can take gettin' accustomed to and probably aren't found in the pages of any dictionary, like "**those'n**" (those people), "**wadn't**" (wasn't), or "**ought'n**" (ought not). By the way, the phrases "**frog strangler**" or "**rainin' cats and dogs**" are slang for a heavy downpour, one that might drown a bullfrog or two.

Another Southern contraction that's guaranteed to be a head-scratcher to those in distant parts is "**sho'nuff**," which is defined as "sure enough" and can be used in the middle of a sentence or as a question at the end: "That young'n sho'nuff knows better'n to mis-behave," or "He misbehaved? Sho'nuff?" In Southern speak, young'n is a variation of young one or youngster.

Both "**ain't a'gonna**" or "**I'm a'tellin' you**" are more Southern con-tractions, translated as "not going to" and "I'm telling you." They both are somewhat akin to double or even triple negatives often used by Southerners for effect. Take the story of a boy who was **actin' out** (misbehavin') in a restaurant because he was **itchin'** (yearnin') for his daddy to buy him a sucker. His daddy reacted with a double nega-tive: "You keep actin' like that, and you ain't never gonna get one."

Unbeknownst to some, the word "**a'tall**" doesn't have a blessed thing to do with height. Suppose you heard someone say this: "Jim Bob doesn't have any sense a'tall." By hearing "a'tall" used in a sen-tence, you probably would determine that it is "at all."

Purty please—and I'm beggin' you—do not make the mistake of equatin' such talk with ignorance or improper upbringin'. Some Southern folks who let a few grammatical rules slip and slide could very well be college graduates who have heard those words all their lives and merely need a good editor to tighten up the way they talk.

If you hear a Southerner say he is gonna "**cut off the lights**" or "**spark to her**," don't think twice about that fellow electrocutin' him-self. "Cut" means turn off, and "spark" means he has an attraction to a **right purty** (pretty) young lady. The Southern word "**tump**" is made up and probably is a combination of tumble and dump, as in: "Don't be a nitwit and tump over the garbage can."

What follows is a list of words and definitions that typically are used in the South. I've also added words that Southerners tend to pronounce a little bit different from other folks.

FIXIN' TO (Gettin' ready to)

*"Kyle is **fixin' to** knock the fool out of that broken-down dryer if it keeps makin' that ruckus."*

MASH (Push)

*"**Mash** the button for the second floor, please."* Or, *"Auntie Lake, how 'bout **mashing** up some potatoes for supper."*

BLESS YOUR HEART (A way to insult someone without being too ugly about it)

*"That skirt is a just a little bit too short for somebody of your generation, Linda Carol. **Bless your heart.**"*

AIN'T (Is not, are not, or am not)

*"My handyman, Richard, used to always say, 'If it **ain't** broke, don't fix it.'"*

A'HOLT (Reach)

*"I've got a stomachache something fierce and need to get **a'holt** of Doc Powers for some castor oil."*

DRESSIN' (Stuffin')

*"For Thanksgiving, Rosa Lee fixes a big, honkin' turkey, a panful of cornbread **dressin'**, sweet potatoes, and green beans."*

- **OLD MONEY** (Inherited riches)

  *"Melinda is marryin' a college boy from Birmingham who hear tell comes from **old money**."*

- **BOONKIE, BOHUNKUS, BE-HIND** (Backside, fanny, derriere)

  *"Daddy's gonna beat your **boonkie** when he finds out who you've been runnin' with tonight."*

- **RIGMAROLE** (Long and complicated process)

  *"You better not believe that confound **rigmarole** Celestine's dishin' out about bein' robbed."*

- **UP** (Unnecessarily follows words like clean, tidy, and straighten)

  *"Let's clean **up** the kitchen and tidy **up** the pantry."*

- **BORRY** (Borrow)

  *"My mama always said, 'Don't **borry** trouble.'"*

- **NEKKID** (Naked)

  *"When Johnny Ray went to see Doc Andrews for a check-up, he had to get **nekkid** before puttin' on one of those nightgowns the nurse hands you."*

● **PREACHER** (Pastor or minister)

*"The **preacher** delivered a right fine sermon last Sunday. It was much better than the week before."*

● **JACKED UP** (Physically stimulated)

*"Bernie cut the grass in record time because he was all **jacked up** on Mountain Dew."*

● **PEE-CAN** (Pecan, a nut that grows on trees in the South)

*"Grab a bag and let's go pick up **pee-cans** over yonder in the pasture."*

● **HALF RUBBER** (A ball game that originated in the South and is played with half of a rubber ball and a cut-off broom or mop stick. It is similar to baseball, but the bases aren't run. It's often played on the beach.)

*"Let's choose sides for **half rubber,** y'all."*

● **HANKERIN'** (Yearnin')

*"I sure do have a **hankerin'** for a bag of pork rinds."*

● **TINKLE, TEE TEE, GO TO THE RESTROOM, POWDER MY NOSE** (Euphemisms a Southern gal might use when she has to go to the bathroom)

*"All that water Gladys drank at supper is gonna make her have to get up all night long to **tinkle**."*

● **HIT THE BUSHES, TAKE A LEAK, GO SEE A MAN ABOUT A HORSE** (Euphemisms a Southern man might use in mixed company when he has to go to the bathroom)

*"'Scuse me, Melissa. I've gotta go **hit the bushes**."*

● **PUNY** (Not up to par)

*"Suzie was feelin' a little **puny** this mornin' so she stayed home from school."*

● **WHATCHA** (What are you)

*"**Whatcha** plannin' to do after supper?"*

● **BREADBASKET** (Stomach)

*"I'm starvin', y'all. My **breadbasket** needs fillin' up."*

● **TALLIT** (Toilet)

*"John Jones is right hefty and done broke the **tallit** when he sat on it."*

● **MOTORSICKLE** (Motorcycle)

*"Leander Jr. rode that **motorsickle** up and down the street like he was Evel Knievel or somebody."*

- ## STEEL MAGNOLIA (A beautiful, strong Southern woman, as well as the title of a movie that took place in the South)

  *"Cilie may have been the baby, but she truly was the **steel magnolia** in the family."*

- ## CLICKER (Television remote)

  *"I swan! That dadgum **clicker** is always gettin' lost under the sofa cushion."*

- ## SI-REEN (Siren)

  *"When Josie Lynn heard the **si-reen**, she was afraid her baby girl had been in an accident."*

- ## OOEY (Ouch)

  *"**Ooey**, Sister, please pull that splinter outta my finger."*

- ## LANE (Alley)

  *"We keep the garbage cans in the **lane** behind the house, hidden by the pink azaleas."*

- ## MIND YOUR MAMA (Obey and respect your elders)

  *"You better **mind your mama,** or you'll be in hot water."*

- ## UPSIDE (On)

  *"Brenda, if you don't stop kickin' Roy's seat, I'm gonna hit you **upside** the head."*

- ## POCKETBOOK (Purse or handbag)

  *"Memaw, do you have any tissues in your **pocketbook**? My nose is runnin' like a leaky faucet."*

- ## PITCHER (Picture)

  *"Laurie Lynn told me just this mornin' that it's **pitcher** day at Sam's school Monday next."*

- ## MIND TO (Thinkin' of doin' something)

  *"Lee Ann's got a **mind to** blister your fanny for not comin' home straight from school."*

- ## DRAWS (Drawers or undergarments)

  *"Put those T-shirts in the chest of **draws** in Daddy's room."* Or, *"Simmer down and keep your **draws** on, Buster."*

- ## BRITCHES (Slacks or trousers)

  *"Tyler, how'd you rip a hole in those **britches**?"*

- ## CRANK (Start)

  *"Go outside and **crank** up the car, Florrie Lee."*

LIGHTNIN' BUGS (Fireflies)

*"Gol-lee, look at those **lightnin' bugs**. Let's catch a bunch of 'em in a Mason jar."*

STOVE UP (Sore)

*"When Lynn stood up after sittin' so long, she was all **stove up** and couldn't hardly move."*

AND ALL, THEN, NOW (Words Southerners like to put at the end of sentences)

*"I went to the park and saw those folks with the funny hair **and all**." Or, "We're goin' down to the river, OK **then?**" Or, "See ya later, **now**."*

DOOHICKEY, THINGAMAJIG, THINGAMA-BOB, WHATSIT, OR WHATCHAMACALLIT (Words used when you either don't know the name of or you can't recall the name of it right at the moment)

*"Bubba, make yourself useful and look in the glove box for that **doohickey** with the instructions on it."*

MOSEY OR MOSEYIN' (Walking at a leisurely pace)

*"Let's call up Gigi and see if she wants to go down to the Walmart to **mosey** around and people watch."*

VARMINTS (Vermin)

*"Look here, now. Be sure the garbage can lid is on good and tight so those gosh-darn **varmints** won't climb in and drag out that hambone."*

DRUTHERS (Preference)

*"If I had my **druthers**, I would've gone to the ballgame with Luke and them."*

LOLLYGAGGIN' (Takin' your time)

*"Mama's gonna spank your fanny if she finds out you've been **lollygaggin'** instead of doing your school lessons."*

PITCH BLACK DARK (Darker than dark)

*"It was **pitch black dark** when I left the picture show."*

TIME (When)

*"Martha Alice spotted you **time** you walked in the screened door with that fresh plate of peanut brittle."*

CATTYWAMPUS (Off kilter, not straight)

*"Earl, please fix that picture, it's hanging **cattywampus** on the living room wall."*

HOKEY (Corny)

*"That song Auntie Minnie hums sure is **hokey**, but it kinda tugs at my heart strings."*

SMART (Hurt)

*"That paper cut on Alice Jo's pinky finger is gonna **smart** when she washes her hands."*

TIZZY (Nervous excitement)

*"Pauline went all into a **tizzy** when she found out she won the golf tunament (tournament)."*

SLAP (Put on)

*"Before we go out to supper I'm gonna **slap** on a little lipstick and rouge."*

SCOOT (Move over)

*"Gosh ah-mighty, Bubba. **Scoot** on over before I fall off the end of the sofa."*

COMMENCIN' (Startin')

*"I was **commencin'** to go to the grocery store before I smashed my finger in the car door."*

WALLY WORLD (Nickname for Walmart)

*"Archie says he needs to go to **Wally World** today to pick up a can of paint."*

TAR-JAY (Nickname for Target)

*"Can you carry Treena to **Tar-jay** later on to see if any throw pillows are on clearance?"*

JACQUES PEN-A (Southern slang for J.C. Penney)

*"I betcha' we can find those red tennis shoes at **Jacques Pen-a** down by the courthouse."*

- **CLOG** (A popular way of dancing in the mountains of North Carolina and Tennessee)

  *"I just love watchin' those boys and girls **clog** because they move their feet so dang fast."*

- **PICKUP** (A truck)

  *"Maude loaded up the **pickup** with a mess of stuff from the garage and hauled it away to the dump."*

- **NO SIREE, BOB.** (An emphatic phrase used after the words yes or no)

  *"**No siree, Bob**, you can't have another slice of pie."*

- **FETCH** (Get)

  *"Milton said he'd **fetch** some take-outs later on for the young'ns to eat for supper."*

- **WHUP** (Whip)

  *"Eula's liable to **whup** your fanny when she sees how you clipped her Confederate jasmine that was lookin' so pretty on the arbor."*

- **BUGGY** (Grocery Cart)

  *"When Mama goes to the grocery store, she always picks up Little Billy and plops him down in the **buggy**."*

- **CARRY** (To drive or move, not literally carry)

  *"Rose said she was going to **carry** her 10-year-old grand baby to the ball game."*

HOLLA OUT THE SCREEN DOOR AND

Tell Bubba to Come On In

Southern Nicknames and Such

Welcome to the Southern family, warts and all, y'all, with the term "**family**" loosely encompassin' both kinfolk and friends, many of whom are given nicknames as soon as they're at the hospital being born and squinchin' their eyes in the light of day.

By introduction, the typical family unit might include Mama, Daddy, brothers, sisters, and more than likely a few additional relatives bunkin' under the same roof. Brother, or Bubba, is usually what everyone calls the oldest son, who may be named after his father. Sister, or Sissy, may be the only daughter or the eldest girl. Other family members might be christened with affectionate and sometimes crazy-soundin' nicknames, Southern appellations that outsiders may not comprehend. Back when I was comin' up (growin' up), my immediate family included **Siddle, Peon, Pessus, Jeanie Peanie Bad Cold, Jay Bird,** and **Kenro the Boho.** I was the baby—the knot at the end of the string—and I was called Possum Cat by Daddy, Pollykins by Mama, and Tootsie by the sisters.

Like I said, boys can be **Bubba**, **Bubber**, or **Junior**, but a Southern tradition handed down through generations is namin' a daughter after her precious mama, something like a junior for a girl. My mother was named for her mother, which is kinda bafflin' because she was the tenth child in a litter of eleven. Mama continued the tradition and named me for her, and likewise, I gave my daughter, Polly, the same name as my mother and me. I've gotta admit that it can be dadburn confusin'.

Double names are popular in the South as well. Oh sure, you hear plenty of standards, such as the first name Mary with a middle name like Ann, Elizabeth, Lynn, Frances, Louise, Sue, Alice, and the like. But Southerners frequently combine nontraditional names like Sue Nell, Nina Kate, Lyla Jo, Maude Alice, and Lillie May and call the girl by both names. My baby daughter, who's twenty-three, has a friend named Ann Darby Smith, whose sister is Lucy Banks Smith. They're called Ann Darby and Lucy Banks and illustrate a time-honored Southern tradition at its best.

Even some men down South are called by double names, like Billy Joe, Bobby Joe, Billy Bob, and Bobby Lee. Southerners also are inclined to burden their offspring with nicknames, which can be conjured up or borrowed from some other source. James can be Jimbo or Killer (true story though he doesn't fit the part), John could be John Boy, Ken might be Beaver, Charles may be Charlie Brown, and Steve might be Steverino. My friend Hudson and his siblings called their daddy "Skeebo," but Hudson can't rightly recall how his daddy acquired that nickname. Skeebo, in turn, gave Hudson the nickname "Muscles" because he was skinny. Makes sense in a Southern sorta way.

Callin' the roll at our family reunion on Daddy's side has always been a lesson in Southern nicknames. I remember how Victoria Lee was Vic, Regina was Reggie, and Louise was Weezie, all descendants of a man named B.J. Cubbedge, who was known by the initials B.J., which also is a decidedly Southern custom—that is, to refer to a man by his initials

Boys who spent their childhood known as Jimmy, Billy, or Joey sometimes decide when they reach a certain age that a shortened version of their names might not sound as juvenile, so they drop the y and become plain ol' Jim, Bill, or Joe. A good number of prominent Southerners, however, didn't follow that trend. Can you imagine if Jimmy Carter had decided he wanted to be Jim? What about the well-known evangelist Billy Graham, who hailed from North Carolina? That mighty fine preacher just wouldn't sound the same if his name were Bill Graham.

Yep, Southern families lean towards sayin's, expressions, and nicknames that certainly might be a mystery to others who aren't lucky enough to be born and reared in the South.

For example, if Sister **gets up with the chickens** (rises before the sun), by the end of the day she may be **slap tuckered out** and have the **mule lip**, meanin' she is extremely tired and poutin' by stickin' out her bottom lip like a mule. Or, she may look like she has been **rode hard and put up wet** (like a sweaty horse).

COMMON NICKNAMES:

Skeeter
Tank
Honey or Honey Pie
Cutie Pie
Sugah, Sugah Plum, or Shug
Sonny or Sonny Boy
Buck or Bucky
Buzz or Buzzy
Chip or Chipper
Chuck
Junior, Trip, and Trey
Punkin'
Scooter
Pee Wee
Baby Doll
Snuffy

If Granddaddy had too much **white lightnin'**, moonshine, 'shine, or bootleg whiskey, he could be described as being in one of three stages of drunkenness: **toe up** (translation: torn up), **knee walkin'** (fallin' down drunk), or **commode huggin'**, which needs no explanation. He also could be snockered, hammered, smashed, three sheets to the wind, drunk as a skunk, drunk as a coot, or drunk as Cooter Brown.

Once I overheard a hoity-toity woman describe her tipsy college coed daughter as being "**overserved**." This was after the young lady leapt up from a table at a restaurant, stumbled outside, and lost her lunch in the azaleas out front. **Bless her heart!**

But that's enough of **cuttin' up** (gossipin') about the blue bloods. Let's talk more about nicknames. Southern grandmother names can be regular-soundin' like Grandmother, Grandmama, Granny, and Nana, but you'll also hear about **Memaw, Big Mama, Mama Lou, Mawmaw, G-Mama**, and plenty of others. Aunts and uncles also play the nickname game. My aunt Frances always signed her greeting cards "**Po' Auntie**" (for poor), although she was a well-respected schoolteacher and principal who made a decent salary. After Sunday dinner, Auntie and the rest of mama's sisters who weren't blessed with their own young'ns would back the car out of the garage, load up the nieces and nephews, and ride out to the cemetery to spruce up the family lot. A trip to the graveyard always meant payin' our respects to our favorite ornate statues, like the life-sized marble one of six-year-old Gracie, who died in the early 1900s.

The aunts used a lot of expressions that they heard from their mama and their Grandma Mason, who was from middle Georgia. I remember one time when Lil said, "**A whistling woman and a crowing hen never comes to a very good end.**" I asked her what it meant, and she said it translated to "be yourself."

Obviously I heard a boatload of Southern expressions from my relatives, but I may have forgotten one or two. I apologize if I missed a few, but there are just so many that the error of my ways can't be helped.

MUCH OBLIGED, MA'AM, I RECKON

I'll Have a Co-Cola

Kitchens and Pie Safes Filled with Love

Like I said, Southerners love to set a spell and tie on the feed-bag, which is a comical phrase I first heard from my friend Billie Jean, who was named for her daddy, Bill. The elder of the Goodwin sisters is Iris Jane, who got her name from both her mama—Big Iris—and her grandmother Janie.

Anyway, I've always thought the phrase "tie on the feedbag" (like you do to a horse) brought to mind such a funny vision. Speakin' of eatin', Southerners sure keep up with the best of 'em when it comes to gobblin' down groceries. Whether it's beef jerky, pork rinds, boiled peanuts, or liver puddin' spread on a soda cracker, food down South is kinda different from anywhere else. First off, let me explain that dinner in the South isn't served at night; it's a hot meal in the middle of the day, and supper is the meal prepared at night. At our house, Mama always described herself as the chief cook and bottlewash, meaning that she did a little bit of this 'n' that while corralin' five children and teachin' them right from wrong.

In our family, we always like to chew the fat—in other words, talk—when we're sittin' around the supper table with the kinfolk and maybe a friend or two. Southerners love to swap stories while passin' around bowlfuls of steamin' hot vegetables like butter beans, black-eyed peas, summer squash, and fried okra. A Southern table also might be loaded down with platters of fried chicken, barbecued pork, and hamburger steaks smothered in Vidalia onion gravy so dadgum good that they'll make you want to slap yo' mama. The bread selection could include buttery biscuits and slices of cornbread fried up in an iron skillet that might have belonged to Grandma. To wash it all down, pitchers of tea will be situated smack dab in the middle of the table.

I just can't get over how well known Southern cooks are in parts near and far. Just think of the tons of cookbooks written by Southerners. I'm sure that in nearly every volume you can get your hands on, there will be recipes for Deep South favorites like cheese straws, redeye gravy, creamed corn, and other vegetables, and loads of sweets like pralines, pecan pie, and banana puddin'.

However, the main ingredient in any recipe prepared by a Southern cook is love because she has an abidin' affection for her family. Her life's goal is making them happy by fryin' and bakin' and settin' everything out on a fine-lookin' table. In the kitchen, a Southern cook might have a pie safe that's been in her family for years. A pie safe is a wooden cabinet with doors that usually are lined with window screen. The cook puts fresh-baked pies and such in the pie safe after she takes them out of the oven. Her pantry is a genuine work of art, with shelves crammed with staples like flour, grits, cornmeal, cornstarch, oatmeal, sugar (granulated, powdered, and confectioners'), bakin' powder, bakin' soda, vanilla extract, and a couple cans of both Carnation evaporated and condensed milk. Over by the can of shortenin' might be jars of Southern favorites like Duke's mayonnaise and Mount Olive pickles, as well as a leftover Maxwell House coffee can that she has recycled to hold tea bags. You will also spy a few small jars of homemade chutney and relish, gifted to her by church friends who put them up themselves, fresh out of the garden.

Sneak a peek in the refrigerator and you might see buttermilk, real butter (as opposed to margarine or oleo), country sausage, and fresh eggs, of course, that were laid by the hens out back in her chicken coop. Sittin' on the counter will be a tin of bacon grease and maybe a brown paper bag filled with warm goober peas (boiled peanuts) that Daddy picked up at the produce stand on his way home from the office.

If and when Southerners go out to a restaurant and order any kind of carbonated beverage, they smile and politely ask the waitress—who may address them as "hon" or "sweetheart"—if they can please have a Coke or Co-Cola. Lord knows a true Southerner will never ever say "soda" or "pop." In North Carolina, they may ask for Cheerwine, or in Tennessee, they'll request an RC Cola. And when they take a pull from one of those bottles, everything's sure to be hunky dory.

Like I said before, words that might be common everywhere else are absolutely not in a Southerner's vocabulary. What is stored in a Southerner's mental file cabinet are plenty of words that describe food and drink and the way those items are served. On many occasions, Southerners use food references when vittles (victuals) aren't even involved. Go figure.

For example: a young girl who didn't just fall off the turnip truck can be sweet as pie (translation: a nice, smart girl). If a woman has grocery store feet or her dogs are tired, her feet and her tootsies (toes) are hurtin'. When a person maintains his or her temperament under extreme pressure, he or she is as cool as a cucumber or cool as the middle seed of a cucumber. In the South, your mama may advise that you will catch more flies with honey than you can with vinegar, which is a reminder that whatever you're doin', you should remember to ask in a nice way because being nice will help you in the long run. If you take your time to accomplish somethin', someone might whine and tell you you're as slow as molasses.

"I do declare, bless your **PEA-PICKIN'** heart!"

"The mayor's argument about the police station
doesn't amount to a **HILL OF BEANS**."

"Mamma, please pour me a glass of **SWEET MILK**."
(Cow's milk)

"Baby Darlene is so sweet, I could just
EAT HER UP WITH A SPOON."

"Kenny thinks he's **THE BEST THING SINCE SLICED BREAD**."

"Our sixth-grade teacher, Mrs. Price, told us one day,
'**DON'T BITE OFF MORE THAN YOU CAN CHEW**.'"

"A girl I used to work with in Atlanta used the phrase
'**OKEY DOKEY, ARTICHOKEY**.'"

"If we have to walk through the woods to get home,
I'm gonna be on you **LIKE WHITE ON RICE**."

"Over there near the big park
were mine and Bobby's **STOMPIN' GROUNDS**."

"Looks like Mrs. Nancy Barnwell is gonna have to apologize
and **EAT CROW**."

"I've been **RUNNIN' AROUND LIKE A CHICKEN WITH ITS
HEAD CUT OFF** gettin' things ready for the **TAILGATE**."
(A tailgate is a picnic before a Southeastern Conference football game.)

"That good-for-nothin' handyman isn't
HITTIN' A LICK AT A SNAKE and is
HANGIN' AROUND HERE LIKE A FLY ON A BISCUIT."
(Bein' lazy and dawdlin')

"I'm **AS FULL AS A TICK** after eatin'
all that turkey and dressin'."
(A tick swells up after suckin' blood from its host, like a dog or a cat.)

"Mae Louise's chicken and dumplin's are **GOODER THAN GRITS**."
(Somethin' that's great)

"Miss Stellise? Can you bring me a **MOON PIE**
and an RC Cola from the corner store?"
(A moon pie is a Southern cookie-like treat made of chocolate,
graham crackers, and marshmallow.)

"I'm so hungry I could EAT THE HORNS OFF A BILLY GOAT." (Famished)

"Johnny Mae is so hungry she could EAT THE HIND END OF A HORSE."

"Bonnie Jean, the past is just that so there's no sense in **CRYIN' OVER SPILT MILK**."

"Come on, Roy Lee! You better **PUT SOME MEAT ON THOSE BONES OR YOU'RE GONNA DRY UP AND BLOW AWAY**."

"People think Mattie Lee is **EAT UP WITH IGNORANCE** (dumb) because she can't tell her left from her right."

"With the flat tire fixed, we're **COOKIN' WITH GAS**."
(Ready to proceed)

"You don't want to go to church? Well, Big Mom will have a **BONE TO PICK WITH YOU**."

"After they finished **RASTLIN'** (wrestlin') at recess, both Bobby and Terry looked like they'd been **CHEWED UP AND SPIT OUT**."

WORDS OF WISDOM SPOKEN BY
Every Dang Southerner

Phrases and Sayin's from Every Whichaway

"**H**old the phone, y'all!**"** Why in the world would someone want to grab on to your cell phone or clutch the telephone receiver? In the South we have humorous expressions that are tied to every-day items and words that make absolutely no sense to others. See if you can figure out some of 'em by readin' the followin' sentences. I'll give you a hint afterwards.

- ## HOLD THE PHONE. (Stop what you're doing.)

  *"**Hold the phone,** everybody; Mary Sue is engaged and has a big ole rock on her finger."*

- ## AXE TO GRIND (Strong personal opinion)

  *"Sarah Ellen has an **axe to grind** with that teacher who read the book about the Civil War."*

- ## ON THE NEST, GOT A BUN IN THE OVEN, IN THE FAMILY WAY (Pregnant)

  *"A little pooch in her belly area tells me that **she's on the nest/got a bun in the oven/in the family way.**"*

- ## FIT TO BE TIED (Angry)

  *"Aunt Maggie Jean was **fit to be tied** with her next-door neighbor when he drove over her camellia bush."*

- ## LET LOOSE OF THAT IDEA (Forget about it, let it go)

  *"Becky Ann couldn't understand why Mr. Pat just couldn't **let loose of that idea.**"*

- ## STINK TO HIGH HEAVENS (Extra smelly)

  *"When that big pot of cabbage boils, it's gonna make the house **stink to high heavens.**"*

CLOSE ENOUGH FOR GOVERNMENT WORK
(Just good enough)

*"When Daddy helped little Lynn with her homework, he said the arithmetic answers he came up with were **close enough for government work**."*

A HITCH IN HIS GETALONG (A problem that affects the ability to walk)

*"Granddaddy's limpin' because he has **a hitch in his getalong**."*

A PAIN IN HER SAWDUST (Reminiscent of a long-ago period when baby dolls were stuffed with sawdust)

*"When Martha Virginia grabbed her midsection, I figured she must have **a pain in her sawdust**."*

BOONIES, BOONDOCKS, STICKS
(Remote, isolated, out in the country)

*"We could go pick up Sue, but she lives way out in the **boonies/boondocks/sticks**."*

HISSY FIT (Temper tantrum)

*"When Mary Jo's beauty parlor appointment was cancelled, she dropped down on the floor and had one heckuva **hissy fit**."*

DUCK FIT (A bit more serious than a hissy fit)

*"Don't take that rattle away from the baby unless you want to see him pitch a **duck fit**."*

THE DEVIL WAS BEATIN' HIS WIFE.
(Rainin' when the sun is shinin')

*That rainstorm yesterday came in the middle of a sunny afternoon, so I figured **the devil was beatin' his wife.**"*

YOU STUDY LONG, YOU STUDY WRONG.
(Don't overthink somethin', or you'll regret it.)

*"Remember to go with the first thing that comes into your head when you're takin' the test because, like Aunt Iris always said, '**You study long, you study wrong.**'"*

HOTTER THAN A TWO-DOLLAR PISTOL
(Hot!)

*"When our window unit went on the blink, the house was **hotter than a two-dollar pistol.**"*

AS HOT AS A JUNE BRIDE ON A FEATHER BED (Not only hot, but very hot)

*"After Virginia mowed the grass in the summer heat, she was **as hot as a June bride on a feather bed.**"*

TOBACCO ROAD (Novelist Erskine Caldwell's book Tobacco Road was about poor Georgia sharecroppers.)

*"That house over yonder with the paint peelin' off looks like **Tobacco Road.**"*

● DON'T GET TOO BIG FOR YOUR BRITCHES.
(Don't let your wealth go to your head because there was a time when you didn't have money.)

*"When you become rich and famous, **don't get too big for your britches** and forget from whence you came."*

● MAKE A PREACHER CUSS (Frustrating)

*"That Anderson woman is so nervy she could **make a preacher cuss.**"*

● PULL THE DOOR TO. (Shut the door.)

*"**Pull that door to** so the flies won't come in."*

● MEDDLIN' (Interferin')

*"Gossipers like Maudine ought to stop **meddlin'** in everybody else's business."*

● USEFUL AS A SCREEN DOOR ON A SUBMARINE (Totally useless)

*"Her good-for-nothin' husband is about as **useful as a screen door on a submarine.**"*

● DON'T MAKE NO NEVERMIND (Doesn't matter)

*"You're late to Sunday school? Don't worry. It **don't make no nevermind** to Miss Pearlie."*

RUN IT UP THE FLAGPOLE (Test an idea)

*"Mary Frances and I couldn't decide whether the menu we liked for the church supper would appeal to everybody, so we decided to **run it up the flagpole**."*

GAVE HIM THE WHAT FOR (Punishment)

*When Daddy found out that Bubba played hooky, he **gave him the what for** and a whippin'."*

IT'LL ALL COME OUT IN THE WASH.
(Everything will be alright.)

*"Don't worry about that bad grade; **it'll all come out in the wash**."*

SIMMER DOWN. (Calm down.)

*"**Simmer down**, now. Don't be mad, because anger sure ain't becomin' to you."*

FLY OFF THE HANDLE (Lose one's temper)

*"Come on, Ike. There's no need to **fly off the handle** just because I told you to ask for directions."*

KICK UP A FUSS (Argue)

*"Hold on a gosh-darn minute. You don't want to **kick up a fuss** with her just because she was runnin' behind."*

● BUSY AS A BUTTON ON A BARN DOOR

(Assumin' that a barn door had buttons, it would be busy because the farmer goes in and out the door so frequently.)

*"When the Ford dealership downtown had a sale, it was as **busy as a button on a barn door**."*

● THE HELL YOU SAY! (I don't believe it.)

*"Lee Ann got a big raise at the sawmill? **The hell you say!**"*

● SAY WHAT? (Say that again.)

*"You've signed up to rastle a bear? **Say what?**"*

● UP TO SNUFF (Up to par)

*"He had a cold and a cough and told his boss he wouldn't be in the office because he wasn't feeling **up to snuff**."*

● HIGHTAIL IT (Move fast like a deer)

*"Uncle Joe said you'd better **hightail it** out of here if you want to get home before sundown."*

● HUSH YOUR MOUTH. (Be quiet.)

*"Be a good girl, now, Geraldine, and **hush your mouth**."*

- **FARMER'S TAN** (Gettin' sunburned like a farmer who works in the fields, with tan lines at the neck and on the arms from wearin' a T-shirt.)

  *"When Darryl took off his shirt to jump in the pond, the girls started pokin' fun at him because he had a **farmer's tan**."*

- **OOPSY DAISY** (Oops)

  *"**Oopsy daisy**, I just about tripped and fell over that pine tree root and nearabout busted my backside."*

- **GOOD UN** (Good one)

  *"After Uncle Arthur told that knee-slappin' hilarious joke, I told him I thought it was a **good 'un**."*

- **GOIN' TO HELL IN A HANDBASKET** (A colorful addition to the expression "goin' to hell")

  *"If Frankie Brown keeps doin' those tricks, he's **goin' to hell in a handbasket**."*

- **MEND FENCES** (Settle differences)

  *"Come on, now. It's time for you and your brother to **mend fences**."*

- **LIKE WATCHIN' PAINT DRY** (A boring activity)

  *"Sittin' through that hour-long program on ancient history was **like watchin' paint dry**."*

- **CAN'T WIN FOR LOSIN'** (Things keep going wrong.)

   *"Sammy Jones's third wife is thinkin' about divorcin' him on account of his gamblin' habits. He just **can't win for losin'.**"*

- **LIKE HE'S SOMEBODY** (A bigshot, pronounced with an emphasis on "body")

   *"Look at him waltzin' in here **like he's somebody.**"*

- **DEEP POCKETS** (Wealthy)

   *"Mr. Garfield sure must have some mighty **deep pockets** in order to keep up that lifestyle."*

- **WITH BELLS ON** (Indicates enthusiasm)

   *"I told Juanita that you and I would be at the baby shower **with bells on.**"*

- **HOW YOU DO GO ON.** (You must be jokin'.)

   *"Oh, Mr. Butler, you think I'm beautiful? **How you do go on.**"*

- **SCOOTER POOTIN'** (Hanging out, riding around)

   *"Let's pick up Bonnie and Betty after school and go **scooter pootin'.**"*

Land Sakes!

WHAT IN TARNATION?

The Emotional Southerner Speaks His Dadblame Mind

When Southerners get a **mad goin' on**, they have a gracious plenty selection of words or expressions that will make their feelings known to God and everybody. Oftentimes, the words or phrases are euphemisms for cuss words because Southerners believe they are closer to heaven than most and therefore wouldn't want to offend the Good Lord (or their mamas and daddies).

Consider these sentences, and see if you can figure out where the bad words should be:

"What the heck?"

"I don't give a rat's behind."

"Kiss my grits."

"A goll-darn shame."

Do you catch my drift?

If a Southerner is angry, he or she might threaten to **snatch you bald headed** or use these phrases in an exasperated tone:

"WHAT IN THE WORLD are you doin' eatin' that ice cream cone so fast? You're gonna get brain freeze!"

"Calm down now, ya hear? I don't want you to GET YOUR FEATHERS RUFFLED."

"GOODNESS GRACIOUS! Get a load of that lopsided fencepost."

"OH, FOR CRYIN' OUT LOUD! Hang up that telephone before it grows to your ear!"

"WHERE IN TARNATION has Daddy gone to now?"

"GEE WILLAKERS! That horror movie done scar't (scared) me half to death."

"GEE MINITY! That quarterback is gonna run all the way down that dadblame field."

"HOLD YOUR HORSES/WHOA MULE and
WAIT A DADGUM/DARN/DURN minute."

"That's **A FINE HOWDY-DO/A HECKUVA NOTE**
after all we've done for him!"

"Oh, **NUTS/SUGAR/SUGAR FOOT**! I forgot to take the sweet
potato casserole out of the oven."

"**YOU'RE GETTIN' ON MY LAST NERVE**!
Go to your room and put away your toys!"

"You've got a concert ticket on the front row at the civic center?
Well, **SHUT MY MOUTH**!" (Shocked and speechless)

"Good gosh, y'all! Benjamin is really mad and
actin' like **HE'S GOT A BURR IN HIS SADDLE**."
(Somethin's botherin' him.)

"Melvin is takin' another date to the prom?
That just **DILLS MY PICKLE**." (Something maddenin')

"**YOU'VE GOT SOME NERVE** callin' me a schemin' polecat
after all I've done for you."

"**SHOOT/SHOOT FIRE**, that chitlin' (chitterling) stew
is as hot as a firecracker."

"**HELL'S BELLS**, Martha Jane!
I done told you not to fool with those Christmas lights!"

"**DAMNATION!** I can't believe you passed
a car on that hairpin curve."

"**I'M GONNA JERK A KNOT IN YOUR TAIL**
if you don't start actin' like you were raised right!"

"Her **SORRY SPECIMEN** of an ex-husband is a
NO COUNT, LOW-RENT individual."

"If Linda Lou asks me to be quiet one more time, I'm gonna tell her to **STICK IT WHERE THE SUN DON'T SHINE.**"

"If you break any of MeMaw's fine china, she'll **KNOCK YOU INTO NEXT WEEK.**"

"**HALE NO**, I ain't never gonna go to that restaurant again!"

"**HALE YEAH**, I'll be comin' back for more of those shrimp 'n' grits."

"**DA-YUM** (damn)! That good-lookin' fella don't know a **DA-YUM** thing about Southern hospitality."

"After puttin' in all that barbed wire, my back hurts like **THE DICKENS.**"

"If Johnny and Lee Roy don't come home on time from the county fair, their daddy is gonna **RAISE HELL/CAIN/SAND.**"

Speakin' of hell (but don't breathe a word to Mama), Southerners have a sterlin' reputation for loyal Sunday school and church attendance and so forth and for puttin' their hard-earned money in the offerin' plate every week. Some denominations in the South regularly hold tent revivals (complete with hellfire preachin'), melodic gospel sings, and most anything else associated with the Good Book. Southerners go to church for Wednesday night suppers, annual homecomin's, circle meetin's, choir practice, dinner on the grounds, brotherhood gatherin's, Bible studies, and most everythin' else in between that's got to do with that ole-time religion.

Maybe that's why some of the states that make up the South are part of the Bible Belt, a region where churches are a dime a dozen and television preachers—good, bad, and screwball—deliver their sermons with fire and brimstone and then sin, repent, and go to jail. Some even get out of the pokey and, Lord help us, start preachin' to the same flock all over again with nary a care on either part.

Some of the sayin's used by Southerners (and Southern writers, for sure) either come straight from the Bible or are paraphrased, borrowed, and tweaked, the way Southerners are wont to do.

Southerners also are right fond of quotes from the Bible or rewritin' scripture to suit a situation.

"WALK AROUND IN THEIR SHOES AND SEE HOW YOU FEEL."

I can't tell you how many times I heard versions of this phrase while growin' up. Officially, the scripture that's nicknamed "the Golden Rule" is Luke 6:31: "Do to others as you would have them do to you." I remember the time one of my Sunday school teachers gave me a wooden ruler with "The Golden Rule" printed on it because I memorized a certain number of books of the Bible.

I've also been privy to catty conversations with sneaky snark cherry-picked from scripture.

Scripture-related Southernisms

●●●●●●●●●●

"Elizabeth Ann is
PREACHIN' TO THE CHOIR
when she tells me that exercise
makes her legs ache."

"I'll be at church
COME HELL OR HIGH WATER."

"She'll be at the hymn-singin' if
THE LORD'S WILLIN' AND
THE CREEK DON'T RISE."

"MAKEUP COVERS A MULTITUDE OF SINS."

A similar Bible verse is 1 Peter 4:8, which says,
"Love covers over a multitude of sins."

"While taking the Black Sheep to task for hangin' around with the wrong crowd, Daddy said, 'LIE DOWN WITH DOGS, YOU GONNA WAKE UP WITH FLEAS.'"

Proverbs 12:26 says, "The righteous choose their friends carefully, but the way of the wicked leads them astray."

"Granny enjoyed being around folks who acted all Christian-like and religiously-speakin', TALKED THE TALK AND WALKED THE WALK."

According to James 1:22:
"But be ye doers of the word, and not hearers only."

"If that snooty woman's got her nose up in the air, Mama says to just KILL HER WITH KINDNESS"

sounds like Matthew 5:44: "Love your enemies, bless them that curse you," or Matthew 5:39: "Whatsoever shall smite thee on thy rightcheek, turn to him the other also."

"Let's bow our heads, hold hands, and pray about it."

Matthew 7:7: "Ask, and it shall be given you; seek, and ye shall find."

Mama used to like to say, "The Lord helps those who help them-selves," but believe it or not, that saying isn't in the Bible. I read somewhere that ancient Greeks said that. Now who would've known?

"If you act bad, expect bad things to happen because YOU REAP WHAT YOU SOW."

That's Galatians 6:7: "Be not deceived; God is not mocked: for whatsoever a man soweth, that shall he also reap."

My paternal grandmother, Ma Powers, was a staunch Southern Baptist who, without even tryin', knocked the fool out of my funny bone. She lived to be a spry ninety-two years old, although she was as deaf as a post and sometimes scared the bejesus out of me because she yelled and I figured she was raisin' Cain about somethin' that was my fault. She didn't drive an automobile, used a cane (her walkin' stick), and always wore dresses, stockin's, and flat canvas shoes that she referred to as her "easy walkers." She also used to tuck a tissue under her watchband to dab the glow off her forehead. (In the South, horses sweat, men perspire, and women glow.) Ma had three children: Bruce, who was called "Brother"; Louise, who was "Sister"; and my father, who was the baby even when he was a grown man.

Everyone in Daddy's family seemed to have been blessed with a healthy sense of humor. Louise liked to say she was born in Egypt and educated in Rome (both place names in Georgia) and happily entertained my cousins and me with her side-splittin' sayin's and her cacklin' laugh. If Louise and Ma were sittin' on the porch in their rockin' chairs and Ma spotted someone walkin' down the street doin' somethin' that she didn't like, she would shake her finger or her cane and point it upwards to heaven: "Lands sakes, look at that boy ridin' his bike on the sidewalk, he sure is a jack," with "jack," or "jackleg," being a substitute for the word "jackass," a word that never would've passed through Ma's lips. And you can bet the farm on that!

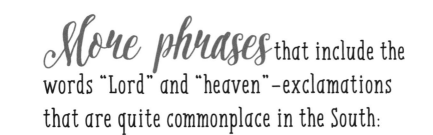

More phrases that include the words "Lord" and "heaven"—exclamations that are quite commonplace in the South:

"LORD/LAWD HAVE MERCY,
that woman's skirt is so short
you can see her credentials!"

"OH, GOOD LORD, what do you think you're doin'
with that pitchfork!"

"GOOD LORD IN HEAVEN,
there's a huge rattler over yonder
by the hosepipe."

"LORD A' MIGHTY, that granddaddy catfish swimmin'
in the pond is as big as a house!"

"**GOTTO MIGHTY**, she sure is as beautiful woman as I've ever seen."

"**GOOD HEAVENS**, she looks as old as the hills and twice as dusty."

"**HEAVENS TO BETSY!** I'm gonna need a stepladder to get in that pickup!"

"**OH, HEAVENLY DAYS!** I miss my mama somethin' powerful."

"**JUMPIN' JEHOSAPHAT!** That boy took off a-runnin' through that cornfield like a bull was chasin' after him!"

"**OH, MY SOUL!** The music program at the mornin' service just made my heart want to sing."

HOW YOU Getting Along?

Fair to Middlin' Greetin's and Salutations

My friend Andy is a college graduate and a successful businessman. He is also what Southerners call a "good ol' boy" because he was born and reared in the South and even told me that he once ate squirrel brains and possum—cooked, of course, and on separate occasions. He told me both of those regional delicacies weren't just good—they were "some kinda good." Andy also is a fellow whose sayin's and stories make me laugh like a hyena. He seasons his conversations with Southernisms, some of which I have never heard in all my years in the South. Dependin' on the time of day, Andy greets someone this way: "Mornin' to ya," or "Evenin' to ya." Once while on a trip to Cuba, he picked up the telephone to talk to a Cuban cigar merchant, and said, "Evenin' to ya," which tickled his travel companions so much that they nearly had a collective conniption fit.

"I liked to have died laughin'," one of his friends told me, using a couple of Southernisms of his own. "I was in the floor laughing my head off."

Andy, like most Southerners, is a friendly cuss and is genuinely interested in the well-bein' of folks. He has relatives from up the country a ways who get a kick out of smilin,' wavin', and **kick-startin'** (initiatin') conversations. They simply love to talk with perfect strangers and delight in visitin' with kinfolk and friends, he said.

The South is overflowin' with a whole lot of greetin's and salutations. If bein' introduced to someone for the first time, a person might say, "**Pleased to meet you.**" If bumpin' into an old friend, the greetin' could be: "**How you been gettin' along?**"; "**What you know good?**"; "**How do?**"; or "**How you doin'?**"

Typical responses may be: "**fair to middlin',**" "**tollable**" for tolerable, "**doin'**" (in response to how you doin'?), or "**as good as can be expected under the circumstances**" if he or she is feelin' poorly.

With such descriptive words to choose from, Southerners tend to be excellent storytellers. They can entertain folks with tales of adventures that might've happened once in a blue moon.

Southern good nights and good-byes are anything but short and sweet, especially when they involve children. Tuckin' a toddler or young child into bed means more than a peck on the cheek and a wish for "**sweet dreams.**" Bedtime in the South is synonymous with a ritual of readin' nursery stories, sayin' prayers, and goin' through a litany of humorous rhyme-times such as: "**Good night, don't let the bed bugs bite**" or "**Night, night, sleep tight.**"

A similar farewell often happens when a Southern college student leaves home to return to school. This time, Mama and Daddy walk the child to the car and say somethin' like, "**Bye, bye, darlin', pick up the telephone and call to let us know you get back, ok?**" As the child backs out of the driveway, he or she watches as the parents continually wave and blow kisses until the car disappears from sight.

Here's an important reminder:

Please don't confuse the word "storytellin'" with stretchin' the truth or lying. A little boy who tells a fib in school might be accused by his teacher of "tellin' a story" or "storyin'." He might have to take home to his mama a note like this, written by his teacher and tucked in his book satchel:

Dear Mrs. Jones,

In class today, Johnny told Billy that he has an alligator in his bathtub. Would you please tell him that it's not a good idea to be storying.

Much obliged,
Mrs. Smith.

A variation of this scenario can occur when company comes for supper. When the host thinks it's time for his friends to leave, he might offer a humorous hint by sayin', "Don't let the screen door hit you on the way out." After a few laughs and a brief story that may start with "That brings to mind the time . . . ," the host and hostess walk the company to the front door and take their time gettin' all the way to the car.

The company might cut the fool (chitchat) for a moment, admire the night sky, discuss the weather ("Sure is a pleasant evenin' . . ."), and once again enthusiastically thank the host and hostess for supper.

When the company gets all situated in the car and the like, the host and hostess continue standin' in the driveway, watchin' and wavin' as their friends drive away.

WE'LL BE THERE DIRECTLY 'CAUSE

Over Yonder is a Fur Piece

Weights, Measures, Comparisons, and Down South Distances

Hearing a Southerner describe a person, place, or thing is like listenin' to a symphony orchestra down to the auditorium (some Southern folks tend to use "to" instead of "at"). You'll hear details like you won't believe, and when you do, you'll be able to paint a picture in your head of exactly what they're talkin' about. If someone is in a **"world of hurt,"** you'll imagine that their pain is as bad as bad can be. If Mama frowns and calls the man who threw litter on the lawn a **"so-and-so,"** you know—**fo' sho**—that a so-and-so is far from a good thing. If a topic is hopeless or too far gone, it may be described as **"too wet to plow."**

For those who do somethin' stupid, a Southerner can choose to describe that sorry so-and-so with one or more of several different phrases, includin':

- "Brother sure is a nice fellow, considering he's **KINDLY BACKWARD**."

- "He's so uncoordinated, he **CAN'T SPIT AND HIT THE GROUND**."

- "That boy who done failed fourth grade twice must be **DUMBER THAN DIRT**."

- "She's as **CRAZY AS A LOON** and **NOT PLAYIN' WITH A FULL DECK**."

- "Bless his heart. Uncle Joe Frank is **ONE BRICK SHY OF A LOAD**."

- "Lenny seems smart, but I'm pert sure **THE PORCH LIGHT IS ON BUT NOBODY'S HOME**."

- "That mistake just goes to show you that she's **NOT THE SHARPEST KNIFE IN THE DRAWER**."

- "He's going about those chores **BASS-ACKWARDS** and **PUTTIN' THE CART BEFORE THE HORSE**." (The pig Latin version of sayin' "ass backwards" and doin' somethin' in the wrong order)

- "Sally, you are actin' like a **NINNY**!" (A foolish person)

- "Al, you are **AS STUBBORN AS A MULE** and **BULL-HEADED TOO!**"

- "With those buck teeth of his, he sure ain't no **PRIZE**."

- "That dyed hair of hers makes her look **AS UGLY AS HOMEMADE SIN**." (Very ugly)

- "He's ridin' that tractor barefooted. He must be **TOUCHED**." (Not in his right mind)

- "When he was a baby, his mama must've dropped him on his head, because he just **AIN'T RIGHT**."

- "Somethin' sure is **OUT OF KILTER** in her mind."

- "I have an old-maid aunt who is as **NUTTY AS A FRUITCAKE**." (A baked good that is filled with nuts. By the way, Claxton, Georgia, is known as the fruitcake capital of the world.)

- "He's so dumb, he **LIVES ABOUT TWENTY MILES OUTSIDE OF RESUME SPEED**."

- She doesn't **HAVE ENOUGH SENSE TO GET OUT OF THE RAIN**."

As far as personal appearances go, Southerners also are known to be a teensy bit cruel. But you can **bet your bottom dollar** that the comments won't be made to anyone's face, and that's a relief. I reckon that hearin' that someone was "**hit with the ugly stick**" or that a person "**fell out of the ugly tree and hit every branch goin' down**" certainly would hurt more than a few feelin's.

However, if someone is **actin' ugly**, it doesn't mean they weren't blessed with a pretty face. Ugly, in this sense, is defined as actin' bad, and a Southerner will tell you in no uncertain terms that "**God don't like ugly.**"

Anger is another emotion that causes Southerners to burst forth with many a colorful expression. For example, if Vernon Junior scribbled on the walls with crayons, Daddy would be so mad he "**could have spit nails.**" If Granny doesn't particularly admire your wardrobe selection, she might tell you that "**you're a sight**"—which is the opposite of a "**sight for sore eyes**," meanin' you're beautiful.

If someone doesn't have many richly goods, he or she "**doesn't have a pot to pee in**" or "is as **poor as a church mouse.**" If that person doesn't have enough money to pay his bills, the collector may shake his head in frustration and declare, "**You can't get blood from a turnip.**"

At the other end of the financial spectrum, sayin' a person is "**in high cotton**" means he is wealthy. But if he is "**high-falootin',**" he is only acting like he's rich.

For crying out loud, what do a few **goll-darn** details matter when you're talkin' about weights, measures, and comparisons? If a summer's day is "**as hot as Hades**," a Southerner will know that you mean it's scorchin' outside without saying the bad *h* word that Mama wouldn't like. If you ask a child for the time, he might tell you it's "**a hair past a freckle eastern elbow time.**" After church that same little boy may go to over to Granny's, who will hug his neck extra tight-like because she hasn't seen him in a "**month of Sundays.**" He absolutely understands where she's comin' from because she hasn't seen him in a "**coon's age.**"

When he steps inside, he realizes that he has time to do a little bit of **piddlin'** before dinner is spread out on the table. Granddaddy might show him how the **frog jumps** and pinch his unprotected bicep. Or, he might share with him how the **crow eats corn** and grab his leg just above the knee and squeeze, while the little boy giggles up a storm.

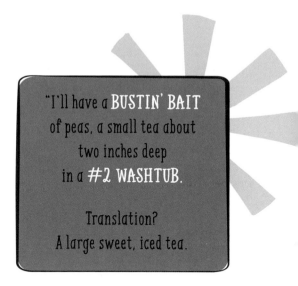

"I'll have a **BUSTIN' BAIT** of peas, a small tea about two inches deep in a **#2 WASHTUB**.

Translation?
A large sweet, iced tea.

Once dinner is ready, he sits down, says the blessing, and lets Granny serve his plate.

NOAH'S ARK AIN'T GOT NOTHIN' ON Southerners

Animals Get In on the Act Too

For reasons unbeknownst to me, Southerners tend to **bark out a barnyard** of sayin's that have somethin' or another to do with animals. A good many expressions are easy to decipher, while others might make you stop dead in your tracks and wonder **what in heaven's name** they mean. If I told you that the **no-see-ums** were horrific down by the marsh, chances are you wouldn't know **what in the Sam Hill** I was talkin' about, so I'll tell you. In the South, no-see-ums are sand gnats that bite you and are so tiny you can't see them. But looka here, those blasted no-see-ums shouldn't at all be confused with **country gnats**, which you *can* see. Country gnats don't bite, but they buzz around your ears and eyes and **just about drive a person to Milledgeville** (the nickname for Georgia's former lunatic asylum that, at one time, was the largest in the world).

No wonder a cow swishes its tail to try to get rid of those annoyin' country gnats! I personally don't believe that Noah invited either kind of gnat on his ark.

Consider these expressions that refer to livin' things:

Expressions that refer to
Livin' things :

- ## A WINK'S AS GOOD AS A NOD TO A BLIND MULE. (Understood a hint)

  *"When Uncle Luther finally told me about the hayloft, I figured out that **a wink's as good as a nod to a blind mule**."*

- ## AS NERVOUS AS A CAT IN A ROOMFUL OF ROCKING CHAIRS (A cat in such a room would be worryin' about its tail gettin' rocked on.)

  *"When Jamie Marie went for the interview, she was **as nervous as a cat in a roomful of rocking chairs**."*

- ## CRAZY AS A LOON (A loon, or coot, has a crazy-soundin' cry, hence the expression.)

  *"Uncle Bubba sometimes acts likes he's as **crazy as a loon** when he steps on the gas in his pickup."*

- ## LOOK WHAT THE CAT DRAGGED IN. (Someone who looks messy and unkempt)

  *"Well, Miss Julie, **look what the cat dragged in**."*

PLAYIN' POSSUM (Pretendin')

*"Judy wasn't sleepin'; she was just **playin' possum**."*

A LITTLE BIRD (A secret source)

*"**A little bird** told me your brother was goin' out with that cute girl who lives around the corner."*

AS LOOSE AS A GOOSE (Totally relaxed)

*"After working out, she was **as loose as a goose**."*

GETS MY GOAT (Annoys)

*"When Grandpa grits his teeth, it really **gets my goat**."*

HOLD YOUR HORSES. (Be patient.)

*"Just **hold your horses**, Glenn, I'm a-comin' right now."*

STUBBORN AS A MULE (Very stubborn)

*"My husband wants to do things his way because he's as **stubborn as a mule**."*

BEE IN YOUR BONNET (Something's bothering you.)

*"You act like you're mad. Do you have a **bee in your bonnet** about missing supper?"*

- ## CAN'T MAKE A SILK PURSE OUT OF A SOW'S EAR (Impossible to make somethin' beautiful out of somethin' that's mediocre, at best)

  *"Forget about slappin' some makeup on Merle because you sure **can't make a silk purse out of a sow's ear.**"*

- ## TIGHTER THAN A GNAT'S FANNY STRETCHED ACROSS A RAIN BARREL (Use your imagination.)

  *"You're so cheap, you're **tighter than a gnat's fanny stretched across a rain barrel.**"*

- ## YOU RUBBED THE BUFFALO OFF THE FIRST NICKEL YOU EVER MADE (Refers to the old-timey buffalo nickel)

  *"You're calling me cheap? **You rubbed the buffalo off the first nickel you ever made.**"*

- ## TOUCHY AS A SETTING OR WET HEN (Sensitive; hens do not like to get wet.)

  *"Why in heaven's name are you cryin' again? You're as **touchy as a setting hen.**"*

  *"When she sassed me, that gal working in customer service at the Walmart made me **madder than a wet hen.**"*

- ## BLEEDIN' LIKE A STUCK PIG (Losin' blood profusely)

  *"After I scratched my knee on the barbed wire, I was **bleedin' like a stuck pig.**"*

- ## TAKE THE BULL BY THE HORNS (Take charge of a situation)

  *"I'm just gonna walk right in that office first thing, and **take the bull by the horns.**"*

- ## THAT DOG SURE WON'T HUNT. (Won't work)

  *"That's the stupidest idea I've ever heard. **That dog sure won't hunt!**"*

- ## IF YOU CAN'T RUN WITH THE BIG DOGS, THEN GET OFF THE PORCH. (Take a risk.)

  *"You don't want to make a bunch of money by sellin' your corn crop to that conglomerate? **If you can't run with the big dogs, then get off the porch.**"*

- ## 'TIL THE COWS COME HOME (A long time)

  *"I'll be lovin' you **'til the cows come home.**"*

- ## GRINNIN' LIKE A POSSUM EATIN' A SWEET POTATO (Smilin' and happy)

  *"After he won that skeet shoot, Papa was **grinnin' like a possum eatin' a sweet potato.**"*

- ## HOG WILD (Eager and excited)

  *"Miss Evelyn is gonna go **hog wild** when she sees all the new inventory down at Clara's Fashion Hub."*

MEANER THAN A BEAR THAT BACKED INTO A BEEHIVE (Provoked and very angry)

*"That policeman who wrote me up for jaywalking was in a bad mood and was **meaner than a bear that backed into a beehive.**"*

AS SNUG AS A BUG IN A RUG (Cozy)

*"When we were sittin' by the fire, we were warm and comfy, **as snug as a bug in a rug.**"*

DON'T COUNT YOUR CHICKENS BEFORE THEY HATCH. (Don't count on anything that hasn't happened yet.)

*"**Don't count your chickens before they hatch** and spend next month's paycheck right now, or you'll definitely have hell to pay."*

THE TAIL WAGS THE DOG (The boss is not in charge.)

*"Tell your coworkers to quit doin' their own thing and start payin' attention to what the boss says, because you definitely don't want **the tail to wag the dog.**"*

ROOSTER TOOT (Nonsensical term for a person actin' like a handful)

*"You're actin' like a little **rooster toot!**"*

- **BIRD** (Strange character or an oddball)

  *"That man paintin' those words on the fence over yonder is a **bird**."*

- **AS BUSY AS A TICK ON A HOUND DOG** (Occupied)

  *"I've had so much paperwork to do, I've been **as busy as a tick on a hound dog**."*

- **TURNED ON ME LIKE A FLOCK OF GEESE** (Mean actin')

  *"Aunt Lillie May was so mad and upset that she **turned on me like a flock of geese**."*

- **WHEN THE CHICKENS COME HOME TO ROOST** (Eventually punished by one's bad deeds)

  *"You'll get your just reward **when the chickens come home to roost**."*

- **CAT HAS BEEN SUCKING ON IT** (Not a good look)

  *"I just woke up and haven't put a brush through my hair yet, so it's gonna look like the **cat has been sucking on it**."*

- **AS HAPPY AS A HOG IN MUD** (Content)

  *"When she was playin' with her grands, she was **as happy as a hog in mud**."*

- ## EVEN A BLIND HOG FINDS AN ACORN NOW AND THEN (Anyone can be lucky.)

  *"You mean to tell me you won the lottery? Well, well, well—I guess **even a blind hog finds an acorn now and then.**"*

- ## FISH OR CUT BAIT. (Get on with business or forget it.)

  *"If he hasn't asked you to marry him yet, just tell him to **fish or cut bait.**"*

- ## LIVIN' HIGH ON THE HOG (Living well and extravagantly; costlier cuts of meat come from higher up on a hog's body.)

  *"With that new car and brand spankin' new house, they are **livin' high on the hog.**"*

- ## AS SURE AS A CAT'S GOT CLIMBIN' GEAR (A sure thing)

  *"Debbie Sue is in the family way **as sure as a cat's got climbin' gear.**"*

- ## PUTTIN' ON THE DOG (A flashy display)

  *"Caroline was **puttin' on the dog** tryin' to impress her boyfriend.*"

- ## SNAKE IN THE GRASS (Sneaky person)

  *"That cheatin' boyfriend of Pam's is just **a snake in the grass.**"*

EGG-SUCKIN' DOG (Someone with a bad habit)

*"After he went out on Lucy again, I told Sonny he was nothin' but an **egg-suckin' dog**."*

LIKE A CAT ON A HOT TIN ROOF
(Nervous, jumpy)

*"Looky here, Janna has been jumpin' around this house **like a cat on a hot tin roof**."*

LIKE PUTTIN' SOCKS ON A ROOSTER
(A difficult task)

*"Attachin' that dryer vent to the hole in the laundry room wall is **like puttin' socks on a rooster**."*

NEKKID AS A JAYBIRD (Stark naked)

*"When that wasp started chasin' Stevie in the shower, he ran out into the bedroom as **nekkid as a jaybird**."*

THERE'S MORE THAN ONE WAY TO SKIN A CAT. (There are other options.)

*"If we can't go thataway to get to town, we'll drive around the mountain because **there's more than one way to skin a cat**."*

LIKE A FISH TO WATER (A natural attraction)

*"Hey, Mama? Daddy told me that when he first met you, he took to you **like a fish to water**."*

MIND YOUR MANNERS, PLEASE AND *Thank You*

Makin' Mama and Daddy Proud as Peacocks

When I was an **itty bitty** thing sittin' around the family supper table, I sometimes would forget where I was and prop up my elbows on the table. As soon as Mama or Daddy called me out, one of my sisters would recite this rhyme in a sing-song voice: **"Mabel, Mabel, strong and able, keep your elbows off the table."**

Good manners at the table and otherwise are all but required in the South. Even before they are **knee high to a grasshopper**, children learn to say "please" and "thank you"; "yes, **ma'am**" and "no, **ma'am**"; "yes, **sir**" and "no, **sir**"; or the abbreviated versions, "yes'm," "no'm," "yessir," or "nossir." It all means the same: respect for parents and elders.

That rule also applies to adults. A Southern gentleman always holds the door for a woman and tips his hat—even a ball cap—to any female that he may encounter. Once inside a building, those hats absolutely should come off. Anyone openin' a door—man or woman—should remember to stop and hold the door for whoever is directly behind them.

The term "Southern belle" first applied to women of the antebellum era who wore hoop skirts and carried parasols. Nowadays, a Southern belle is a true lady who knows her manners backwards, forwards, and sideways.

When a woman enters a room to join a group of friends that includes men, the men should stand, although the woman usually waves her hand and advises them to "please, keep your seats." While strollin' down the street with a woman, a man walks closest to the street—a gesture of respect that I always heard stemmed from horse-and-buggy days when a horse might step in a mud puddle and splash the couple. I guess it's better for the man to be muddy-upped than the woman.

When passin' someone on the street, a man or a woman smiles, makes eye contact, and says hello. A former newspaper society section editor (yes, that's what it once was called) told me that good manners mean makin' others feel comfortable. Write thank-you notes on monogrammed notepaper, and send cards for good cheer and condolence. In this day and age, manners mean promptly respondin' to invitations, e-mails, and telephone calls.

If a Southerner is invited to a small gatherin' or a hen party (women only) at someone's house, she should carry with her a hostess gift, such as a bag of mints or a small container of cheese straws.

Proper funeral etiquette also is a must in the South, although I admit some things have changed in recent years. A straightforward newspaper obituary seems to have gone by the wayside for many folks, although those with a good upbringin'—thank the good Lord—still know the right way to compose a tasteful obit.

For the love of Pete, do not go all dramatic in the write-up and say he "had his transition," "entered into eternal rest," "departed this earthly world," or incorporate some other euphemism. Just say the person died and list his education, accomplishments, memberships, and survivors, followed by the visitation, funeral, and remembrances. Period. Don't go on and on and say she liked to weave potholders or watch the Atlanta Braves on the TV.

Make yourself useful when you hear that a relative of a good friend has died. As soon as you get word, gather together some funeral food: chicken salad or a ham (with Co-Cola or orange juice poured over it before baking to cut the grease). Also good are disposable containers filled with enough macaroni and cheese to feed an army, deviled eggs, a pan of brownies, or a cake with six or more skinny layers iced with caramel or chocolate.

I discovered this tip a few years ago when I was shoppin' at the Goodwill. An older woman confided to me that she buys plates there to put the funeral food on so the bereaved won't have to worry about returnin' her china. Lord knows, the mourners will have plenty to do without frettin' about gettin' a plate back to its rightful owner in a timely manner.

Ask a friend or relative to be in charge of an unspoken committee of women who will skip the cemetery and go back to the house or the church social hall to set the food on the tables for family and friends.

Have flowers delivered to the house so mourners can enjoy them and realize that they're in your thoughts. An arrangement sent to the funeral home is mighty nice, but take it from me, those expensive flower buds are gonna die a quick death in the blazin' hot sun in the cemetery. Trust me on that one.

Mail a handwritten note and share a detailed memory of the person, such as, "I remember the time your mama took the time to come visit with me while I was laid up in the hospital with that naggin' ankle sprain. I'll never forget all of her kindnesses."

Wearin' clothes that your mama would approve of means you were raised right as well. In the summertime it's perfectly alright for men to wear seersucker suits, starched shirts with button-down collars, and white buck shoes. If a man has a mind to, he can pick out a bow tie from the closet, just like my sweet daddy did for most of his adult years. (He lived 'til the ripe old age of ninety-five and had a mind as sharp as a tack and all his wits about him.)

But that's enough sentimental stuff for right now. Lemme return to fashion sense in the South. As far as overalls go, farmers or railroad workers should be the only ones who wear them, y'all. For cryin' out loud, those movie stars and celebrities who gallivant about in overalls just don't understand the function and practicality of a good pair of denim overalls. First of all, they can be worn over street clothes for protection from spills or tears. Secondly, overalls have a **passel** of **handy-dandy** pockets, straps, and loops to hold tools and whatnot. Since when did they become fashion statements?

Both men and women should remember that even though society has relaxed fashion rules, it's in good taste for men to wear a coat and tie to church and for women to put on a dress. Wearing anything less formal is about as tacky as having guitars, drums, and big old television screens in churches. Now don't get me started on that!

Women who work outside of the home should choose dresses or skirts of a decent length, slacks, and close-toed shoes. If wearin' a blouse with a skirt or appropriate pants, a woman should remember not to expose her décolletage for all the old biddies in the office to see and gab about around the water fountain. Proper undergarments also are a must. If a slip is necessary, make sure it's not **snowin' down South**, which means your slip is showin'.

Casually, Southern women are akin to the rest of the world, unfortunately, and nowadays are puttin' on most anything and everything when it comes to fashion. A true Southern woman or girl will have respect for both herself and her mama and wear tasteful clothes.

Other clothin' and related expressions that might be seen or heard in the South include these:

FASHIONABLE *Southernisms*

- ## PEDAL PUSHERS (Often called capris)
  *"Lula Bell? Go put on your **pedal pushers**, and we'll go for a walk down to the store."*

- ## TENNIS SHOES (All athletic shoes)
  *"A big ol' blister came up on my toe after I wore out my **tennis shoes** climbin' up those red clay hills in north Georgia."*

- ## STOCKIN'S (Not hose)
  *"Nancy Kay has a run in her **stockin's**. Run upstairs and get the clear fingernail polish out of my bureau so we can stop it from runnin' any more."*

- ## BLUE JEANS (Not just jeans)
  *"Get on your **blue jeans**, and come help me pull those weeds out of the garden."*

- ## BLOUSE (Not a top or shirt)
  *"Aunt Ernestine was wearin' a lovely **blouse** with that skirt you gave her for her last birthday."*

- **HIGH WATERS** (Slacks or trousers that are too short)

  *"Looka there at Jim Bob. He grew so tall over the winter that his suit pants are **high waters**."*

- **GET YOUR PANTIES IN A WAD** (Get mad)

  *"Don't **get your panties in a wad** just 'cause Junior is going bowlin'."*

- **KEEP YOUR SHORTS ON** (Be patient.)

  *"**Keep your shorts on**, Bubba. The Tigers will score in a minute."*

- **BELLYACHIN'** (Complaining)

  *"Quit your **bellyachin'** Norma Jean. Put your big girl pants on and get over it."*

CITIES AND TOWNS THAT'LL JUST

Tickle Your Gizzard

Place Names that You Just Won't Believe

I don't live but a **hop, skip, and a jump** from Santa Claus, Georgia: a **speck in the road** that seems like it's just a neighborhood, but it's **sho'nuff** a place where I hear you can have a letter to the man himself postmarked "Santa Claus." One time I was drivin' near there—for what, the reason escapes me now—and decided to ride on through. I was tickled when I saw thoroughfares with names like Candy Cane Lane, December Drive, Sleigh and Noel Streets, and Dasher, Dancer, and Rudolph Way. Oddly enough, I even saw a Salem Street in Santa Claus.

Santa Claus isn't necessarily a Southern name for a town because there's a Santa Claus, Indiana, but here's a collection of towns and cities in the South with names that you won't believe but are sure to make you smile. Take the town of Between, Georgia, which is between Athens and Atlanta. Makes perfect sense, doesn't it?

Try these other Georgia places on for size:

● ● ● ● ● ● ● ● ●

Hopeulikit
Experiment
Climax
Unadilla*
Luthersville
Sparta
Athens
Rome
Egypt

*not to be confused
with an armadillo

South Carolina has more than a few interesting-sounding towns:

● ● ● ● ● ● ● ●

Happy Bottom
Ninety-Six
Quarantine
Spiderweb
Tickle Hill
Wide Awake

In Mississippi, you'll find:

• • • • • • • • •

Possumneck
Chickenbone
Alligator
Whynot
Sanatorium

How 'bout these Alabama cities and towns:

• • • • • • • • •

Beehive
Burnt Corn
Normal
Lick Skillet
Slicklizzard
Gobblers Crossing
Frog Eye
Chigger Hill
Smut Eye
Scarce Grease

North Carolina also has some amusin' place names:
● ● ● ● ● ● ● ●
Boogertown
Lizard Lick
Climax
Bat Cave
Poor Town
Tickbite

Louisiana certainly has a bunch of sweet-soundin' places:
● ● ● ● ● ● ● ●
Uneedus
Bunkie
Frogmore
Coochie
Waggaman
Belcher

Take me to Tennessee to find these towns:
● ● ● ● ● ● ● ●
Sweet Lips
Stinking Creek
Turtletown
Flippin'
Goat City
Ducktown
Bugtussle
Nankip

MY DEAR, IT'S ALL IN DEM BOOKS, TV SHOWS, *Movies, and Music*

Storytellers Who Can Draw, Write, Sing, and Make Us Laugh

In the living room of my house stands a tall, glass-front armoire that once was in the front hall at my grandparents' home in the country. It's a drop-dead gorgeous piece of furniture filled with a few precious items that I have collected through the years, as well as a good many family heirlooms. Though they're not worth much monetarily speakin', these treasures are riches to me.

On one shelf are a half dozen books written by my father's first cousin, a woman named Willie Snow Ethridge, who was the daughter of my great aunt Missy, whose proper name was Georgia. I met Willie when I was a little girl and knew a smidgeon about her but never fully appreciated her literary talents until I started readin' her nonfiction books. Some might describe Willie as a Southern Erma Bombeck, a humorist who wrote about the vicissitudes of life with her family.

A few of Willie's books were handed down to me by my grand-mother Ma, who was Willie's aunt (if you care to climb my family tree). Willie always presented Ma with one of her books and wrote a note inside the front cover beginnin' with Ma's other nickname, which was Darly Mag. Why was she called Darly? Heaven knows. It could have been because a child or her sister couldn't pronounce "darlin'," which often is how nicknames are born.

Not too long ago, I opened up the doors of that armoire and picked out Willie's book *As I Live and Breathe*, a title that in itself is a Southernism meanin' an expression of surprise at comin' across someone or somethin' unexpectedly. In this particular book, published in 1925, Willie tells tales on her newspaper husband and their three small children, nicknamed Shug, Bubber, and her third child, whom she calls "the Youngest Offspring."

Willie's witty writin' is a wonderful example of Southern prose. No brag, just fact. Consider this description of Shug: "She is tall, broad-shouldered and decidedly chubby. When polite people see her, they say, 'Oh, what a fine, healthy-looking girl!' When her uncles see her, they say, 'It is a shame your mother and father took the feedbag from you so soon, isn't it, child?' And with sly winks they call her 'Puny.'"

This excerpt just oozes with Southern style: "These first days of summer also mean light, cold suppers with a salad of sliced toma-toes and bell peppers and cucumbers and lettuce and a platter of sliced roast beef or fried chicken and a dessert of iced watermelon or peaches."

Boastin' aside about my own kin, I think some of the most glo-rious examples of Southernisms come from the pages of books and stories written by other authors from Georgia, as well as those from all the nooks and crannies of the Deep South. Think of a handful of best-sellin' books and their creators, and you won't have to read far at all before you come across a collection of thoughts knitted together so beautifully that you wonder how on God's green earth anybody could conjure up those magical words. I like to believe it's because they were raised in the South and were gifted with a keen ear to pick up the vernacular of relatives, neighbors, and friends.

In my book of favorites, Margaret Mitchell tops the list of authors and writers who knew how to describe the South and its people during the Civil War. Mitchell's only book, *Gone with the Wind*, is well known as the quintessential Southern novel. I was in the seventh grade when I was introduced to Mitchell's unforgettable couple, Scarlett O'Hara and Rhett Butler (be still my beating heart). Later, I was spending the night with my friend Kay, who was totally immersed in *GWTW* and life at Tara—the O'Haras' homeplace—when I closed my eyes and dozed off. When I awoke, I saw that Kay Mallette Exley—her middle name comes from her daddy's side of the family—was still readin' and holdin' on to every word. She and I waited with bated breath for the re-release of the 1939 film so we could see all those beloved characters at the picture show, as my daddy called the movie theater. The epic film was long, which necessitated an intermission at the dramatic part where Scarlett pulls a carrot out of the ground, shakes it at the skies, and declares, "As God as my witness, I will never be hungry again."

QUOTES FROM

Gone with the Wind

"**FRANKLY,** my dear, I don't give a damn."
(This is perhaps the most famous quote from *GWTW*
and spoken by Rhett to Scarlett.)

"I'll think about that tomorrow.
After all, tomorrow is another day."

"You'd rather live with that silly little fool who can't open
her mouth except to say 'yes' or 'no' and raise a **PASSEL OF
MEALY-MOUTHED BRATS** just like her."

"**FIDDLE**-dee-dee."

"I don't know **NOTHIN' 'BOUT BIRTHIN'** babies."

"I'm **GWINE** to Atlanta and **GWINE** to Atlanta I is."

MARGARET MITCHELL,
GONE WITH THE WIND, 1936

Over in Columbus, Georgia, a woman named Carson McCullers became a writer of short stories, novels, and plays—a collection of material that introduced generations of readers throughout the world to Southern-speak. McCullers's style has been categorized as Southern Gothic, a genre that focuses on misfits or damaged characters.

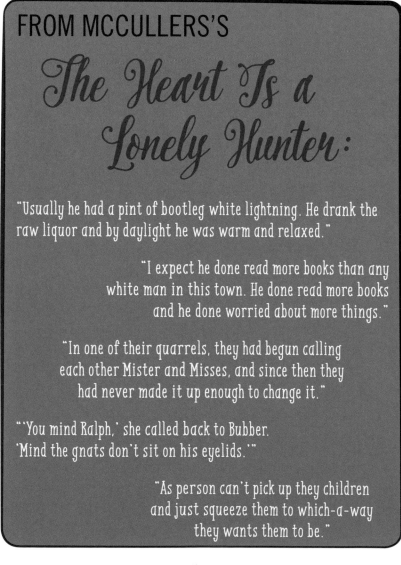

FROM MCCULLERS'S

The Heart Is a Lonely Hunter:

"Usually he had a pint of bootleg white lightning. He drank the raw liquor and by daylight he was warm and relaxed."

"I expect he done read more books than any white man in this town. He done read more books and he done worried about more things."

"In one of their quarrels, they had begun calling each other Mister and Misses, and since then they had never made it up enough to change it."

"'You mind Ralph,' she called back to Bubber. 'Mind the gnats don't sit on his eyelids.'"

"As person can't pick up they children and just squeeze them to which-a-way they wants them to be."

Flannery O'Connor was a short story writer who also focused on Southern Gothic, which she explained thisaway: "Whenever I'm asked why Southern writers particularly have a penchant for writing about freaks, I say it is because we are still able to recognize one."

O'Connor was born in my hometown of Savannah, Georgia; and the house where she lived until she was twelve is now a museum within the confines of the city's historic district.

A few beauts
from some of O'Connor's short stories:

"'She would've been a good woman,' said The Misfit, 'if it had been somebody there to shoot her every minute of her life.'"

"You shall know the truth and the truth shall make you odd."

"Faith is what someone knows to be true, whether they believe it or not."

"He and the girl had almost nothing to say to each other. One thing he did say was 'I ain't got any tattoo on my back.' 'What you got on it?' the girl said. 'My shirt,' Parker said. 'Haw.' 'Haw, haw,' the girl said politely."

"Her name was Maude and she drank whisky all day from a fruit jar under the counter."

Alice Walker is an African-American author who was the youngest of eight children born to sharecroppers in Putnam County, Georgia, which is in middle Georgia and encompasses the city of Eatonton. She is probably best known for her Pulitzer Prize–winnin' novel *The Color Purple*, which was made into a successful movie.

Note the Southern sound of these passages from *The Color Purple:*

> "I ain't never struck a living thing, I say.
> Oh, when I was at home I tap the little ones on the behind
> to make 'em behave, but not hard enough to hurt."

> "Everything want to be loved.
> Us sing and dance and holler, just trying to be loved."

> "His little whistle sound like it lost way down a jar,
> and the jar in the bottom of the creek."

> "What will people say, you running off to Memphis like
> you don't have a house to look after?"

> "Sofia the kind of woman no matter what she have in her
> hand she make it look like a weapon."

Joel Chandler Harris, who created the famous Southern characters Uncle Remus and Br'er Rabbit, among others, was born in Eatonton but was part of an earlier generation than Walker. Harris once was an associate editor at the *Savannah Morning News,* the place where I first was employed as a writer. In fact, Harris's rockin' chair is roped off and sittin' in the publisher's office at the newspaper.

Harris spent time on a plantation, where he heard African American workers share stories. As a result, it is said that he modeled characters such as Uncle Remus after some of the people he knew. He wrote the Uncle Remus stories to "preserve in permanent shape those

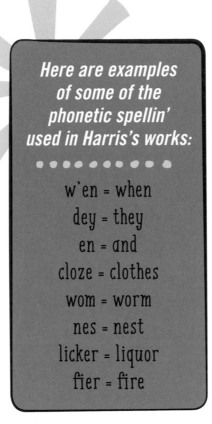

Here are examples of some of the phonetic spellin' used in Harris's works:

w'en = when

dey = they

en = and

cloze = clothes

wom = worm

nes = nest

licker = liquor

fier = fire

curious mementoes of a period that will no doubt be sadly misrepresented by historians of the future," accordin' to Bruce Bickley in the book *Nights with Uncle Remus.* Although widely criticized for the dialect he used in his writin', Harris was purported to be a supporter of equal rights for African Americans.

Alabama has its share of authors who also use plenty of Southernisms in their books and short stories. Harper Lee of Monroeville wrote *To Kill a Mockingbird*, a Pulitzer Prize–winnin' novel set in the fictitious town of Maycomb, Alabama, and a book that I can read over and over again.

EXCERPTS FROM

To Kill a Mockingbird

"Real courage is when you know you're licked
before you begin, but you begin anyway and
see it through no matter what."

"I think there's just one kind of folks. Folks."

"You can choose your friends but you sho' can't choose
your family, an' they're still kin to you no matter
whether you acknowledge 'em or not, and it makes you
look right silly when you don't."

"Miss Jean Louise, stand up. Your father's passin'."

Truman Capote was a colleague and friend of Lee's and wrote the critically acclaimed true crime book *In Cold Blood,* as well as short stories such as *Breakfast at Tiffany's* and *A Christmas Memory,* a seasonal favorite that's filled with Southern language and descriptions.

FROM TRUMAN CAPOTE'S
A Christmas Memory

"I've always thought a body would have to be sick and dying before they saw the Lord."

"My friend has never been to a picture show, nor does she intend to: 'I'd rather hear you tell the story, Buddy. That way I can imagine it more. Besides, a person my age shouldn't squander their eyes. When the Lord comes, let me see him clear.'"

"It's fruitcake weather!"

Just like the writers who came before him, Pulitzer Prize–winnin' author Rick Bragg is a prime example of a Southerner who has leaned on his growin'-up experiences to put words to paper. He was born in northeastern Alabama and grew up in Possum Trot, and to me, that fact alone makes him Southern as all get out. When I read his books, I think he might've said somethin' like this when he wrote them: **"You bet your bottom dollar I'm from the South."**

Check out these quotes and see for yourself:

QUOTES BY
Rick Bragg

"It was a good moment, the kind you would like to press between the pages of a book, or hide in your sock drawer, so you could say it again."

"If you cannot eat what you want in the South, life is not worth living."

"I guess it is what you do if you grow up with warnings of damnation ringing from every church door and radio station and family reunion, in a place where total strangers will walk up to you at the Piggly Wiggly and ask if you are saved."

"You can dream on welfare. You can hope as you take in ironing. It is just less painful if you don't."

"These were people . . . who built redwood decks on their mobile homes and have no idea that smart-aleck Yankees think that is somehow funny. People of the pines. My people."

Fannie Flagg quotes:

● ● ● ● ● ● ● ● ● ●

"You know, a heart can be broken, but it keeps on a-beating, just the same."

"Face it, girls. I'm older and I have more insurance."

"Are you a politician, or does lying just run in your family?"

"I believe in God but I don't believe you have to go crazy to prove it."

Many people heard Alabama native Fannie Flagg use quirky Southernisms when she used to appear on various television programs. Those days were long before she began writin' books with colorful titles like *Fried Green Tomatoes at the Whistle Stop Café* and *Welcome to the World, Baby Girl!* No doubt, Flagg collected some of her book material in her native Alabama.

Mississippi's William Faulkner wrote dozens of books and stories both before and after he won the 1949 Nobel Prize for Literature. Purists of prose consider him one of the best writers—not just Southern— who walked this earth. Like many Southern wordsmiths, his style was influenced by his family, particularly his mother, maternal grandmother, and the African American woman who tended to him as a child.

Also from Mississippi is Eudora Welty, whose novel *The Optimist's Daughter* won the 1973 Pulitzer Prize. Welty studied advertising at Columbia University and, as her first real job, worked at a radio station. She then worked in the society section of the Jackson, Mississippi, newspaper before going out on her own to write short stories and novels. (My first job was at a radio station, followed by a position in the society section of the *Savannah Morning News*.) Welty once was quoted as saying, "Southerners love a good tale. They are born reciters, great memory retainers, diary keepers, letter exchangers   great talkers."

quotes from some of Faulkner's works:

"I feel like a wet seed wild in the hot blind earth."

"My, my. A body does get around. Here we ain't been coming from Alabama but two months, and now it's already Tennessee."

"Be scared. You can't help that. But don't be afraid. Ain't nothing in the woods going to hurt you unless you corner it, or it smells that you are afraid."

"Sometimes I think it ain't none of us pure crazy and ain't none of us pure sane until the balance of us talks him that-a-way."

"A mule will work for you ten years for the privilege of kicking you once."

"Between what did happen and what ought to happened, I don't never have trouble picking ought."

HERE ARE A FEW EXAMPLES FROM

Eudora Welty's
literary library:

"People are mostly layers of violence and tenderness wrapped like bulbs, and it is difficult to say what makes them onions or hyacinths."

"Up home we loved a good storm coming, we'd fly outdoors and run up and down to meet it."

"Come one of these nights and we can wander down here and tree a nice possum. Old Jack Frost will be pinching things up. Old Mr. Winter will be standing in the door . . ."

"In the end, it takes phenomenal neatness of housekeeping to put it through the heads of men that they are swine."

"They've got these pygmies down there, too, an' Mrs. Pike was just wild about 'em. You know, the teeniniest men in the universe? Well, honey, they can just rest back on their little bohunkus an' roll around an' you can't hardly tell if they're sittin' or standin'."

Fine books aren't the only things that get the literary juices flowin' in Southerners or those folks who can write and pretend they're from down yonder.

Way back when, a few creative types stumbled upon Southern slang and found out that sharin' it made people laugh. It wasn't long before Southern references and characters were found in the funny papers, on television, in the movies, and all over tarnation.

In the early 1940s, a comic strip called *Pogo* was created by a cartoonist named Walt Kelly and was set in the Okefenokee Swamp near Waycross, Georgia. Pogo the possum and Albert the alligator, along with a bunch of their animal buddies, came to life, and the comic strip soon was picked up and syndicated, which introduced Pogo and his "swamp-speak" to readers throughout the United States and the world.

Eventually, some of the hilarious made-up words and phrases created by Kelly—such as the use of "done" before a verb—crept into the American lexicon. No doubt, Pogo and the conversations he had with his pals were modeled after language used and heard in the rural South. Two months after his death, the following quote from the strip was used to honor Kelly: "Don't take life so serious, son. It ain't nohow permanent."

Here are some more sayin's from Pogo that helped put the South on the entertainment map:

"Halp! My powerful brain is blowed itself up!"

"Some is more equal than others, as is well known. It ain't that your majority is outnumbered, you're just out-surrounded."

Way before Pogo took center stage in Georgia's swamp, *Lil Abner* made its debut in the funnies. Cartoonist Al Capp created a clan of hillbillies who lived in and around the fictional Dogpatch, which was supposed to be in Kentucky.

HERE ARE A FEW QUOTES FROM
Lil Abner
THAT'LL GET YA GRINNIN':

"I looked in the mirror this mornin' and most of my good years are gone."

"Romeo Scragg, do you claim to be Daisy Mae's kith an' kin?"

"You gals are going to have to go through a before-marriage custom called 'engagement.'"

"[Engagement is] the part before the gal says, 'Shore do!' and the preacher says, 'Go to.'"

"Good is better than evil because it's nicer!"

Pretty soon television hopped on the Southern bandwagon, and in the early 1960s, networks began runnin' situation comedies set in the South. I bet you can name shows on all ten of your fingers in which the characters talk with a twang or a drawl and recite lines that will ring a Southern bell (not to be confused with a Southern belle). Here are some of my favorite shows with a few quotes on the side:

The Andy Griffith Show:

"It's up to the love bug whether he's gonna love or not."

"I keep gettin' my britches caught on my own pitchfork."

"Daylight's precious when you're a young'n."

"Well, you and Aunt Bee is havin' fried chicken
and I'm havin' crow."

"Nip it, nip it in the bud."

The Beverly Hillbillies:

"That's cause I grad-ge-ated the six grade, ma'am, only took three
years."

"If brains was lead, that boy wouldn't have
enough grease to grease a skillet."

"How do you like your possum, Lowell, fallin' off the bones tender
or with a little fightin' left in it."

"She's from one of those fer'n nations."

Green Acres:

"You look prettier than a catfish with his nose stuck up against a dam."

"Learnin' to like wallpaper is like pushin' a purple straw through a keyhole."

"I don't know what you do in New York, but around here we don't give a man a funeral unless we're pretty sure he needs one."

"Yessir, at Haney's Farm Mindin' Service, for a nom-yew-nal fee we will move into yer house, eat yer food, drink your likker, and turn away any unwanted relatives that might show up at yer door."

Hee Haw:

"Hey, Granpa. What's for supper? Here's what's on the menu tonight. Baked possum, sweet 'taters, turnip greens, Indian pie, corn cake, pickled beets, and crumb pudding.'"

"I'd marry a preacher so I could be good for nothing."

"Claustrophobia is a dreaded fear of Santa Claus."

"Junior, I read in the paper that up in New York City a man gets hit by a car every thirty minutes. Lord, I bet he's gettin' tired of that by now."

The Dukes of Hazzard:

"The Duke boys done gone in the pond."

"Enos, you just proved it. You ain't got enough smarts
to cover a frog's eyelashes."

"I'm gonna cuff ya and stuff ya."

"That J.D. Hogg is more crooked than a dog's hind leg."

"Judas priest on a pony."

"Come on, Rosco, get in.
We'll drive you all the way to the pearly gates."

Designing Women:

"Yeah, well, I donate to the ASPCA, but that doesn't make me a cat."

"I'm sayin' this is the South. And we're proud of our crazy people.
We don't hide them up in the attic. We bring 'em right down
to the livin' room and show 'em off."

"Out, out of my house! As God as my witness,
I will burn it down myself before I let you in again."

Duck Dynasty:

"Where I come from, you don't mess with another man's woman or his hat."

"Do me a favor and shut your yapper."

"When I hear a sound that's particularly unpleasant I gotta put a stop to it."

Through the years, the South has looked good, bad, and butt ugly on the silver screen. Now, I'm askin' you, how could anybody possibly forget some of the lines said in the movies that have been set in the South? I'll tell you one thing, though: I'd sure like to dismiss from my mind some of the God-awful, pathetic Southern accents I've heard while munchin' on my popcorn at the picture show. Lawd, have mercy on my soul! Nevertheless, here are a few Southern movies and quotes that my family, friends, and I remember from goin' to the show:

A Streetcar Named Desire:

"I have always depended on the kindness of strangers."

"When your sister first met me, she thought I was common. Well, I'm common alright, common as dirt."

"A cultivated woman—a woman of breeding and intelligence—can enrich a man's life immeasurably."

All the King's Men:

"I don't need money. People gives me things because they believe in me."

"I'm the hick they were gonna use to split the hick vote. But I'm standing right here now on my hind legs. Even a dog can learn to do that!"

"You don't prosecute an addin' machine if a spring goes busted and makes a mistake."

Deliverance:

"Where you goin', city boy?"

"Right there's the town hall. Right over there's the little old fire station. Played a lot of checkers over there, sure did."

"Night has fallen. And there's nothin' we can do about it."

Steel Magnolias:

"Well, we went skinny dippin' and we did things that frightened the fish."

"Sammy's so confused he don't know whether to scratch his watch or wind his butt."

"The only reason people are nice to me is because I have more money than God."

"I was there when that wonderful creature drifted into my life and I was there when she drifted out. It was the most precious moment of my life."

Driving Miss Daisy:

"Sometimes I think you ain't got the sense God gave a lemon."

"I taught some of the stupidest children God ever put on the face of this earth ..."

"Lord, I tell you one thing...she sho' know how to throw a fit."

"I wouldn't be in your shoes if the sweet Lord Jesus came down and asked me himself."

"Say she done gone around the bend a little bit. Well now, that'll happen as they get on."

Mississippi Burning:

"You have to be a member to drink here."

"Down here they say rattlesnakes don't commit suicide."

"It's ugly. This whole thing is so ugly."

"Y'all think you can drive any ol' speed down here."

Sweet Home Alabama:

"I just kept thinkin', 'Oh preacher, hurry up before he changes his mind.' Now that man makes me so crazy sometimes I could wring his neck."

"I can't control her anymore, any more than I can control the weather."

"Hi honey! Lookin' good. How's the family?"

Walk the Line:

"John, I have a casserole in the oven and your sister in the kitchen, and I don't wanna talk about the tour."

"You've got me all revved up. Now I've asked you forty different ways and it's time you come up with a fresh answer."

"Don't give me no rules! All I got are rules."

Talladega Nights: The Ballad of Ricky Bobby:

"The field mouse is fast, but the owl eats at night."

"Ricky Bobby appears to be unhurt, but that Wonder Bread car is toast."

"If you ain't first, you're last."

Forrest Gump:

"Life is like a box of chocolates.
You never know whatcha gonna get."

"Stupid is as stupid does."

"Jenny and me was like peas and carrots."

"I was a national celebrity famouser than
Captain Kangaroo."

Comedians found out a long time ago that makin' fun of the South and Southerners would get an audience laughin' and snortin' **faster than green grass through a goose.** Those that make fun of the South come from all parts of the country, but the finest comedians, in my opinion, are the ones who were raised in the region and deliver their one-liners with authentic Southern accents.

Jerry Clower was born in Liberty, Mississippi (pronounced MISS-sippi), and told such entertaining stories that he decided to go on the lecture circuit. He also performed at the Grand Ole Opry and was nicknamed "the Mouth of Mississippi."

JERRY CLOWER

Record Albums:

"Country Ham"
"Ain't God Good"
"More Good 'Uns"
"Peaches and Possums"

Words and Phrases:

"They got to
noticin' me…"

"Growed up
in the country…"

"Want it some kind
of bad…"

"They's all settin'
around the table…"

"I blow'd the lamp
out…"

"Boogered me up bad…"

Minnie Pearl was from Tennessee and, like Clower, appeared at the Grand Ole Opry. With the price tag hangin' from her straw hat, she also was a fixture on *Hee Haw*. Her albums included *Howdy* and *Lookin' for a Feller*.

A FEW JOKES BY

Minnie Pearl:

"Marriage is like a hot bath.
Once you get used to it, it ain't so hot."

"One of those handsome Secret Service fellas
frisked me all up and down, so I turned
around and went out and back in again."

"The doctor must have put my pacemaker in wrong.
Every time my husband kisses me,
the garage door opens up."

Lewis Grizzard, who hailed from Georgia, got his start in the newspaper business but branched out into writin' books and performin' stand-up comedy.

Books written by Grizzard include humorous titles like *Won't You Come Home, Billy Bob Bailey*; *Don't Sit Under the Grits Tree with Anyone Else but Me*; *If Love Were Oil, I'd Be About a Quart Low*; and *Chili Dawgs Always Bark at Night*.

LEWIS GRIZZARD'S
Southern-fried quotes

"It's difficult to think anything but pleasant thoughts while eating a homegrown tomato."

"What we can do in the South is we can take a word and change it just a little bit and make it mean something altogether different."

"If you want something sweet, order the pound cake. Anybody who puts sugar in the cornbread is a heathen who doesn't love the Lord, not to mention Southeastern Conference football."

"There's no such thing as being too Southern."

"There's a big difference between the words 'naked' and 'nekkid.' Naked means you don't have any clothes on and nekkid means you don't have any clothes on and you're up to something."

Although Roy Blount Jr. was born in Indiana, his family moved to Atlanta, where he was raised, which, in my book, qualifies him as a Southerner. He wrote for *Sports Illustrated* magazine for several years before writin' a bunch of books as well as goin' on the lecture circuit.

The Southern music scene means country, of course, but also includes good ol' Southern gospel. Many a country artist has recorded collections of hymns and gospel songs. And I can't possibly forget the genre of Southern rock music that emerged during the 1970s with the likes of the Allman Brothers, the Marshall Tucker Band, and Lynard Skynard, to name just a few.

Lemme start with country music, which is durn near like prose, complete with flowery similes and metaphors and plenty of Southern-isms. There are more than a few songs with down-home lyrics and a handful of gospel tunes that might make you want to get down on your knees and give thanks.

Roy Blount Jr. quotes:

"Certainly people have said a lot of deeply unfortunate and stupid things in Southern accents, but that doesn't mean there's anything wrong with the accent itself."

"The North isn't a place. It's just a direction out of the South."

"People may think of Southern humor in terms of missing teeth and outhouse accidents, but the best of it is a rich vein running through the best of Southern literature."

Down-Home Lyrics:

"Hoverin' by my suitcase tryin' to find a warm place to spend the night. A heavy rain a fallin' seems I hear your voice callin'... a rainy night in Georgia ... I believe it's rainin' all over the world."

"My father was a gambler down in Georgia, he wound up on the wrong end of a gun. And I was born in the backseat of a Greyhound bus, rollin' down Highway 41."

"I ain't never been with a woman long enough for my boots to get old. We've been together so long now they both need to be sewed. If I ever settled down, you'd be my kind, and it's a good time for me to head on down the line."

QUOTES FROM
Country Songs

"Hey, hey good lookin' **WHATCHA GOT COOKIN'**?"

"Where I come from it's cornbread and chicken.
Where I come from it's a lotta **FRONT PORCH PICKIN'**."

"Big wheels keep on turning, carry me home to see my kin.
Singing songs about the south-land. I miss **'OLE' 'BAMY** once
again and I think it's a sin."

"We got married in a fever, **HOTTER THAN A PEPPER SPROUT**.
We've been talkin' about Jackson ever since the fire went out."

"Them old Mason jars that Daddy made us wash and
SET THEM OUT TO SUN on our back porch … "

"We've got chicken every Sunday and the preacher comes around.
And every Saturday mornin' Daddy takes us all to town. And we'll
go to the **PICTURE SHOW** or picnics on the ground."

"You left my heart
AS EMPTY AS A MONDAY MORNING CHURCH."

"Hold the door, say please,
say thank you. Don't steal.
Don't cheat."

"She's **GOT A BODY LIKE A $100 BILL**, soft as satin, smooth as silk. And to top all that, she's got a heart to match."

"I drive a pickup truck and
I don't pass the buck.
And I always speak my mind."

"We loaded up my old station wagon with a tent, Coleman and sleepin' bags. Some fishin' poles, a cooler of Coke ..."

"She's too cute to **GET ON MY LAST NERVE.**"

"Those city lights drew you like a magnet.
You were attracted to his **HIGH-FALOOTIN'** crowd."

"All day long we work in the fields. Then bring it on home to a
home cooked meal. **WE LOVE YA LIKE SUNDAY, TREAT
YA LIKE SATURDAY NIGHT.** And when the bed gets full we can
sleep in the hay. We're from the country and we like it that way."

"And my house, it's not much to talk about,
but it's filled with love that's grown in
Southern ground-and a **LITTLE BIT
OF CHICKEN FRIED.**"

"'Cause I've got friends in low places,
where the whiskey drowns and the beer chases
my blues away, and I'll be okay."

Soulful lines

from Southern gospel music:

"I don't ask you, Lord, to lighten up my burden.
I don't mind the trials on Earth that I go through.
Being down I want to prove that I am worthy of
a little spot of heaven close to you."

"I'll fly away, oh glory, I'll fly away.
When I die, Hallelujah, by and by I'll fly away."

"When the roll is called up yonder, I'll be there."

"You saw me cryin' in the chapel.
The tears I shed were tears of joy.
I know the meaning of contentment.
I am happy with the Lord."

"There will be peace in the valley for me, someday.
There will be peace in the valley for me, oh Lord, I pray.
There'll be no sadness, no sorrow, no trouble I see.
There will be peace in the valley for me, for me."

So there you have it, y'all. I've given you Southernisms for most every occasion and more. Feel free to share these sayin's with good friends, as well as a few enemies too. Just like my precious mama used to tell me, "Kill 'em with kindness, baby girl, and be sweet."

Until next time,

Bless your heart and mind your mama.

Bye, now!

About the Author

POLLY POWERS STRAMM is a veteran journalist who has written and/or coauthored eight books including *Uncle Bubba's Savannah Seafood, Savannah's Historic Neighborhoods, Sentimental Savannah, Our Savannah, Mr. Dickey's Barbecue, St. Patrick's Day in Savannah, Walking Tours of Old Savannah,* and *Savannah: Crown of the Colonial Coast.* She is also a longtime newspaper reporter whose column "Polly's People" appears in the *Savannah Morning News.*

Polly is a graduate of the University of Georgia ("Go Dawgs") and achieved a lifelong dream years ago when she was asked to be a stringer for *People Magazine.* By far, though, her greatest accomplishment is her precious family—her husband, Steve, and daughters, Little Polly (married to son-in-law, Tyler Carver) and Mary. Both of Polly and Steve's daughters are registered nurses, which Polly Sr. knows brings a smile to the face of her "Doctor" Daddy up in heaven.